Are you Ready ?
Carol Spieckerman

Nice Car

"Ready, Set... Whoa!"

Are You Really Ready for Retailers?

By

Lisa Carver & Carol Spieckerman

authorHOUSE™

1663 LIBERTY DRIVE, SUITE 200
BLOOMINGTON, INDIANA 47403
(800) 839-8640
WWW.AUTHORHOUSE.COM

First published by AuthorHouse 07/26/05

ISBN: 1-4208-1403-6 (e)
ISBN: 1-4208-1404-4 (sc)

Library of Congress Control Number: 2004099376

Printed in the United States of America
Bloomington, Indiana

This book is printed on acid-free paper.

Table of Contents

Disclaimer

This book was written to provide information regarding doing better business with major retailers. The text of this book should be used as a general guide and you are urged to read all of the available material and learn as much as possible about manufacturing and retail. Every effort has been made to make this book as complete and accurate as possible. However, there may be mistakes, both typographical and in content, and information and resources contained in this book are current only up to the date of printing.

This book was written with the understanding that the publisher and authors are not rendering legal, accounting, or other professional services. If legal or other expert assistance is required, the services of a professional should be sought.

The purpose of this book is to educate and entertain. The authors shall have neither the liability or responsibility to any persona or entity with respect to loss or damages caused, alleged to have been caused, directly or indirectly, by the information contained in this book.

Introduction

Who are "Pencils"?

Pencils make buying and placement decisions that affect the revenue of your company and your company's eligibility for retail and licensing opportunities. Your Pencil may be a retail buyer, assistant buyer, merchandise manager, or licensor.

What is the Pencil Principle?

That "Products Fail Without Performance"

In today's retail environment, suppliers must position themselves as logical destinations for opportunities through innovation, execution, service, and an understanding of their Pencil's business. While your products may still get you in the door, they will not secure your long-term advantage.

Who will benefit from the Pencil Principle series?

■ Start-up supplier companies that want to develop an understanding of modern major retail and licensing processes.

- Start-up supplier companies that are seeking reality-based strategies which will make the best use of available resources.

- Start-up supplier companies that want to assess the viability of retail launch.

- Established vendor companies that are concerned about hitting a wall with their current accounts and licensing partners.

- All vendor companies that desire to become candidates for new branding, licensing, and distribution opportunities.

- All vendor companies that seek to maintain long-term advantages with their current and future retail and licensing partners.

Unlike the multitude of traditional one-size-fits-all business and sales tomes, the Pencil Principle series was created to specifically address the needs of suppliers to major retailers and beyond that, we focus on major retailer and licensor expectations ("Big Pencils"). Our assumption is that once you are meeting and exceeding the expectations of the most sophisticated retailers and licensors, you are generally well positioned to take excellent care of everyone else.

The Pencil Principle series spotlights approaches and techniques that apply to both start-up and established vendor companies. We believe that start-up companies will benefit from looking one step ahead at the challenges facing established suppliers, while established vendors can continue to explore best practices. That said, the most beneficial information for established suppliers begins in Chapter Five although we believe that you will find helpful and entertaining information throughout the book. After all, growing established suppliers find themselves in a "start-up" position any time they seek to launch new products or expand distribution! Beyond that, much of the information in Chapter Two, Five, and Six, as well as Chapters Eight through Eighteen, borrow from our sales seminars and can be used by established suppliers to smooth out the rough edges and re-visit successful sales strategies and follow-up techniques.

The Pencil Principle series does not claim to provide magic bullets that will guarantee initial buyer meetings for start-ups (no one can do that), or to eradicate the most onerous and inevitable conflicts between Pencils and their vendors (mark-downs, co-op requests, late shipments, and tight schedules). For established companies, we explore non-product best practices that increase face-time and alleviate problems while improving the perception of your company in the eyes of your most valued Pencils.

Getting retail distribution can be challenging but losing it is easy. Are you ready?

Terms

We will use the term "vendor" and "supplier" interchangeably.

Pencil Points

Summarize previously-covered topics.

Pencil Pearls

Illustrative stories from our experience.

May this book serve as a reality-based guide for distributing your products in today's competitive retail marketplace.

Chapter 1: Really?

The New Pencil Paradigm

Power has completely shifted in the last decade from the vendor to the Pencil.

We remember the days when Pencils lined up outside of showroom doors during busy market weeks just to see the latest. In most cases, the appointments were fairly leisurely, personal affairs in which your Pencil would carefully consider your product (over catered breakfast or lunch), ask for your input and recommendations, and, if you were really hot, write orders on the spot (or at least drop them by your showroom by the end of market). From there, everyone would go out for cocktails and dinner and do their best to make it through another day of market the following day. Such was the level of trust back then that Carol used to devote the better part of a week to writing orders *for* several of her department store buyers (at their request).

In those days, it was also feasible for a cold call to pay off with an initial appointment. Today, you are more likely to find yourself filling out supplier applications, sending samples in advance, or following other gate-keeping procedures in hopes of obtaining an initial meeting with a Pencil.

Industry trade shows once provided the best opportunity for start-ups to get noticed. Now, major Pencils continue to move their buying calendars back. Traditional trade-show timing is often out of synch with Pencil buying seasons; and retailers no longer rely on trade show attendance to view products (they expect products to be brought to their corporate offices).

The Sophistication Chasm

Over the past decade, major retailers have become a force to be reckoned with, bringing sales volumes, door counts, and licensing program placements that were unimaginable ten years ago. Many start-up suppliers and even some established vendors assume that this just spells more revenue potential with no inherent change in their processes. Nothing could be further from the truth.

With increased volume has come an exponential increase in sophistication and retailer back-office support (departmental analysts, assistants assigned to focus on smaller segments of business, and proprietary vendor-managed systems). Additionally, retail Pencils are outsourcing more functions to their suppliers in order to cut costs. As a result, suppliers are no longer just selling products, they are taking on pieces of their Pencil's administrative responsibilities and co-managing their Pencil's business. The retailers' corresponding expectation of sophistication at the vendor level is often not met and can be difficult for even seasoned vendors to achieve.

Pencil Point # 1

Pencil organizations have become quite complex and, as a result, selling to major Pencils has never required more skill.

Shrinking Vendor Base

Start-up companies can tend to believe that all they need is the next great idea or "must have" product in order to gain widespread retail distribution. The fact is that it has never been easier for Pencils to source products on their own, and they are more determined than ever to shrink their supplier base.

At the same time, our assessment work continues to confirm that retailers are experiencing a great deal of frustration with their existing suppliers. Top retailers are constantly upgrading their skills via corporately-endorsed training programs, yet most vendor companies possess no internal training programs whatsoever. As a result, many suppliers have stagnated or fallen behind as their retailers have become more sophisticated.

In spite of buyer frustration with existing suppliers, Pencils tell us they would still rather empower their existing vendor base or source products directly than continually add new, untested suppliers, particularly those providing only one or two items. This is especially true in light of quota phase-outs in some categories which make direct-sourcing even more attractive to retailers.

This trend has evolved in sharp contrast to the previous practice of doing business with a wide variety of suppliers so as to lessen dependence and increase product variety.

Pencil Pearl

One buyer recently summed up his thoughts at a "top ten" departmental meeting within a major mass retailer (in which the top ten vendors for that department meet to discuss strategy) this way: "Get big or get out ..." and "If you can't fill a truck now, think about how you can in the future."

Pencil Point # 2

Pencils are committed to doing more business with fewer suppliers (rather than seeking new product resources).

More than ever, suppliers need to offer a compelling "reason to be" (see Chapter 10) and a corresponding "reason to buy" for the Pencil. Moreover, companies must think beyond initial placement and into maintaining their initial advantage by perfecting execution and continually expanding their offerings in order to stay on the radar.

Now that you know the obstacles, let's talk about strategy!

Chapter 2: The Four "First Things First" Questions

The following are the four questions that we suggest all of our start-up clients consider before pursuing retail distribution. Answering them provides an early reality check and sets the stage for a logical approach to distribution. They also serve as a "refresher" for established companies.

Question # 1: Who Is My Primary Customer and How Will It Change My Approach?

Many start-up companies base their ventures on a fundamentally flawed premise, that their customer will be the *consumer*. While the consumer is definitely the "end user" of a supplier company's products, the supplier's primary customer is the *retail buyer* (the Pencil).

Assume that while it will always be necessary to stay abreast of consumer trends in order to remain meaningful to retailers, planning your launch and ongoing business from the retailer's perspective will be of primary importance.

Working from this premise will drastically change your approach to product, packaging, and pricing. For example:

- Your product and packaging will be designed with your target retailer's current programs in mind and will change in order to accommodate specific retailer requests. Your product will not be designed as "one size fits all" since each retailer has unique pricing, packaging, branding, and presentation standards.

- Your product dimensions will most likely be determined by your target retailer's fixture dimensions and/or dimensions of similar products, not by what you think is cute, trendy, or even practical.

- Your product's pricing will be based on your target retailer's pricing structure, not on what you think someone would pay or on what you believe your profit should be.

While the Pencil is your primary customer, knowledge of consumer trends and how they support your product(s) is a key element of your product story. The trick is to present this information without appearing to presume to know the Pencil's customer better than she does.

We see this problem of presumption come up more and more in our consulting practice, even with established high-end suppliers that are attempting to expand their distribution into mass or dollar store retailers. We are astounded when established vendors make comments like, "We know that your customer doesn't expect the same high quality..." or, "Considering that most of your customers are minorities ..." in first meetings with discounter-Pencils. No

Pencil wants to hear a vendor underestimate or make ill-informed assumptions about their customer! Whether he buys for a dollar store or a luxury retailer, every Pencil is seeking the highest quality at the most advantageous price for their customers. Pencils also usually possess far more sophisticated tools than most suppliers do for discerning the make-up of their customers. Leave those assumptions to the Pencil.

Pencil Point # 3

The Pencil, not the consumer, is your primary customer.

Question # 2: Who Is the "Customer Within the Customer"?

Just as there are differences among individual retailers, there are also different buying structures within each retailer. A specialty store may have one owner who is also the Pencil for the store; a small chain may have four to five Pencils who cover various categories within the store group; a department store may have many more; and a mass retailer may have hundreds of Pencils who buy very specific categories-within-categories.

While it is difficult to know each retailer's buying structure without some kind of inside knowledge, you can develop a general idea of how items are bought within a department by observing retail ticketing within the stores (noting e.g. department numbers, categories, and/or sub categories), or by purchasing current buyer directories.

7

In general, the larger the store group, the larger your range of options for placement and possibilities for approaching more than one Pencil with your product.

Pencil Point # 4

No two retail buying structures are exactly the same.

Question # 3: How Can I Research and Refine My Concept?

We often have to remind start-ups, and even established companies, that running a product by their sister and her friends who "love to shop" is not true market research. Market research, conducted by a reputable and industry-aware consultant, is a powerful and objective tool for bolstering your product story. In general, Pencils will listen to market research and find it interesting if presented logically and within context. On the other hand, some of our clients conduct market research solely to deepen their knowledge of their products, brands, pricing, and competition without ever directly mentioning the research to their Pencils.

It is alarming how even established vendors waste tremendous product development resources by taking a stab at a new product launch or line extension. Start-up companies that make an early investment in market research not only benefit from crucial product fine-tuning early in the game, they put their best foot forward in initial Pencil meetings by lessening the chance of wasting a valuable presentation.

Market research can include:

Competitive landscape analysis, in which information regarding competitive pricing, packaging, and distribution is determined.

Market space assessments, in which the market space for your product category is determined.

Strategic price point research, to obtain an overview of existing price points in your category by class-of-trade.

Consumer research, where focus groups or individual consumer interviews are conducted to determine consumer receptivity and response to packaging, pricing, and/or brand.

Pencil Pearl

A start-up consumer electronics company came to us with a truly revolutionary product. They saw it as a "natural" for mass retail (and of course, the promise of thousands of doors of initial distribution fueled this assumption)! By the time they came to us, they had  spent upwards of a quarter million dollars on product development for this feature-rich product. They considered the product to be ready for retail even though they had designed and priced it in a complete vacuum (the "build it and they will come" mentality). After conducting a thorough competitive landscape analysis for them, it was clear that the retail price points they needed to achieve were completely out of line with those of their targeted retailers. Our client had also made assumptions regarding the safety and durability of the product without having it tested. We went on to conduct a series of consumer panels for them, testing usability, pricing, and features. The panels revealed that consumers were happy to do without many of the bells and whistles in order to bring the price down and also showed that a closet market existed for adult consumers (the product was initially thought to appeal only to teenagers). The product modifications and corresponding cost reductions resulted in a truly retail-ready product that was later presented, and successfully tested, in a major mass retailer. The Pencil appreciated the supplier's revisions based on market research and agreed that the price was right. He was enlightened by the findings regarding older consumers at a time when he was considering adding more "adult" offerings to his product mix.

Question # 4: Is It "Missing" or "Not Meant to Be"?

In our consulting practice, we receive several inquiries each week from start-up companies that decided to launch a product based solely on an *assumption* about what is "missing" in the market.

We often hear some version of, "I noticed that there weren't any product X, in the stores and decided to make one ..." or, "I've always thought someone should make a product X." Many validate the premise further via friends' opinions that the item is viable and indeed cannot be found in the market. This logic, even when completely accurate, is often a faulty premise for a retail launch. Why? Because products can be excluded from manufacturing and distribution for any number of reasons including:

- The price of the item exceeds the highest price points in that product's logical department (i.e., a ceramic bowl that would need to retail for $30.00 when the high-volume price point for bowls in the home department for the targeted retailer is $9.99).

- The item is embellished or "forward" when the targeted department does a high percentage of its business in basics (i.e., a ceramic bowl that is hand-painted with intricate patterns when 90% of the Pencil's business is done in solid-colored glass bowls).

- The item would cannibalize sales of an already-successful item (i.e., a set of four ceramic bowls that would take sales away from super-successful bowls sold individually at a higher margin).

- The item has already been tried and it failed (the Pencil placed an order for ceramic bowls last year and sales were terrible).

- The Pencil is in the process of sourcing a similar product with another supplier or sourcing it directly.

It can be difficult to know for sure which, if any, of these scenarios is at work, but we encourage you to look deeper and consider the Pencil-centric reasons for your product launch while anticipating potential Pencil objections.

This requires exploring product in the stores, conducting competitive landscape and other market research, and maintaining an ongoing willingness to change your product, pricing, and packaging. If you are simply seeking sales for a product *as is,* consider targeting specialty stores or pursuing alternative venues such as eBay (and we often recommend this as a viable alternative for our start-up clients).

Pencil Point # 5

If your product isn't currently in the market, you owe it to yourself to find out why before committing resources.

Now let's drill down on the Pencil-centric reasons-to-be for your product and specific standards for seeking a retail meeting.

Chapter 3: What Is Your Pencil-Centric Premise?

As mentioned before, we are contacted by many, many people who have an idea that they believe fills a void and is a natural for retail distribution or licensing. Going back to the preceding chapters, there was a time when products were regularly "discovered," when orders were literally "written," and when buyers "bought." Plenty of people believe that is how business is still done, and they therefore aspire to getting just one Pencil presentation scheduled for their product(s). They are convinced that once the Pencils see the product, they will become so enamored that an all-store order will be written on the spot. Beyond that, they assume that those orders will immediately generate profit. We don't mean to sound condescending, but it is astounding how many people invest their life savings before realizing that this just *isn't* the way it works.

We will start once again by playing devil's advocate and then move into viable strategies for start-ups. Generally speaking, aspiring suppliers must realize that an *idea* is not a product, nor is it a license until it has been manufactured or is at least represented by a well-crafted prototype that is able to be manufactured. Secondly, as pointed out before, the chances of launching one hot item with a major retailer are increasingly rare since most of them are making it their goal to do *more* business with *fewer* suppliers and they generally will not invest their time on one-hit wonders.

Pencil Point # 6

You will have to have more than just an idea in order to approach a Pencil.

How Viable Is It?

Your chances of getting major distribution for your products increase exponentially if they meet the following standards:

- The product has documented success with well-respected specialty stores, chains, or e-commerce companies.
- You are able to present a family of items that tell a compelling story when merchandised together (not a one-hit wonder).
- You are presenting an item or group of items that offer a clear price or quality advantage over products the retailer is currently carrying.
- Your product uniquely addresses a hot trend.
- You have managed to become a licensee for a license that is corporately supported by the retailer.

On the last point, it is important to note that individual Pencils do not generally make licensing decisions. Major licensing initiatives are launched at the corporate level and implemented by individual Pencils.

Established and aspiring suppliers are often surprised when they realize their Pencils don't necessarily *want* "higher quality" products. As items wear out, they must be replaced and this of course drives sales. And, there are many categories of products for which price, not quality, will always be the ultimate consideration. Therefore, betting your success on quality alone can be short-sighted.

Pricing from a Pencil Perspective

As consultants, we often hear one of the following assumptions regarding how new products should be priced:

- The aspiring supplier has spent more money than anticipated on various combinations of packaging, lawyers, trade show exhibits, product development, and ill-advised overhead, and therefore decides that the product must retail at a certain price.

- The aspiring supplier has not researched the market to determine not only what price points are out there in a given category and retail distribution, but which price points are the volume price points for a given category or retail department.

Again contrasting the old days with the new, many people don't realize that these days the retailer sets the retail. That isn't to say they won't take your input into consideration (based on success with similar retailers, for example) or that a few categories of product operate under set retails (major brand cosmetics, for example).

The mistake that many suppliers make (this includes those with established businesses), is to take a "Based on my investment/overhead, they need to put this out at $9.99" approach. Consider this: What if 80% of the retailer's business in your item or category is done at $7.99 and only 3% of their business is done above that price point? All retailers also have different pricing structures, retail price "endings" (literally, the ending or "cents" part of a retail price which varies between retailers), and product mixes. This illustrates why having a professional competitive landscape analysis for a given retailer is so important.

Don't make it your goal to *convince* a given retailer to place a product that is completely out of their pricing structure. It is not only unrealistic, but would be a shallow victory if achieved. Pricing your product out of your retailer's departmental price range will at best decrease overall sales for your product and, at worst, get your product kicked out when it proves to be less productive than other items in that department. You are better off targeting a retailer who can tolerate the higher price point, going back to the drawing board to take out features and get your price down, or deciding whether you can fit into their retail structure and work on lower margins. We have worked with many established suppliers who continue to try and push prices up without considering the overall volume consequences and the impact on their reputation and longevity with the retailer.

You should also assume that the price of your products will only go *down* from initial cost and plan your pricing accordingly. Established suppliers are often challenged to *reduce* prices each year since major retailers expect that the volume they bring to a supplier company will achieve price-lowering economies of scale. Beyond that, practices such as reverse auctions and plain old competition ensure that achieving price increases is nearly impossible unless features have been added to your product that will justify an increase.

Pencil Point # 7

Product pricing is a strategic process and the highest price often is not the best price for the Pencil OR for you.

When discussing pricing with your Pencil, you should focus on your *cost* (your price to the retailer), not the Pencil's *retail* (the cost to the consumer), which is largely out of your control. Suppliers who go into retailers talking "needed retail" are immediately pegged as amateurs. In order to talk retail at all, you must refer to the retails in that Pencil's department, i.e., "Marcie, I really believe that this would sell wonderfully on your $9.99 rounder fixture and at our cost of $5.00, that will give you a 50% mark-up ..." or, "This would be a natural as an accessory topper display above your private label knit pants." The goal is not necessarily to get the highest price, the goal is to get the most volume and that often means *lowering* the price strategically.

Retailers also operate on different "mark-ups" (the difference between the cost and the retail or: Retail minus Cost divided by Retail, expressed as a percentage.

Some retailers (many department stores for example), use a lot of promotional pricing – they begin with retails on the "high" (55% or higher) then offer progressive promotions and discounts until the product is sold out. Discount mass retailers operate under "EDLP" (every day low pricing), with lower initial mark-ups (depending on the category, 30–45% or lower), and less promotional activity. It is interesting to note that many discounters are currently testing better brand offerings in order to achieve higher initial mark-ups and retails. The hope is that this "good, better, best" strategy will lure better shoppers and of course, that higher profits will be realized.

Pencil Pearl

In a market landscape assessment that we conducted for a client, we discovered that all of their products were priced in the top 10% of retail price points of every store group and department in which they had become so committed to keeping their prices up that they were missing out on a tremendous amount of volume.

The client went on to select several products for price reduction and presented the reductions to their Pencils. Not only did the Pencils appreciate the reduced cost, the resulting lower retails (no more than a 10% reduction) garnered a 30% volume increase for the supplier!

We aren't pretending to offer a full retail math course in this chapter (we've only TOUCHED on various aspects of pricing and placement), but we do want to drive home the need for research and for qualified assistance when planning any foray into retail distribution.

Pencil Point # 8

When planning product placement and pricing, do your research and bring in qualified help.

newmarketbuilders' "Are You Really Ready for Retailers?" Checklist

Beyond the above considerations, you should not attempt to meet with a major Pencil until you can clearly and honestly answer the following questions:

- What is my capacity (how many of these items can I produce at a given time)?
- What is my current inventory (do I have any items on hand right now and, if so, how many)?
- What is my lead time (how quickly can I get items shipped to the Pencil and how many)?
- What is my pricing structure (what is the lowest cost to the Pencil that I can offer while still making my desired

margin)? You want to know how low you can go in price negotiations while still making margin.

- Who will I be competing with within this retailer and what are my points of differentiation?

- If this item is not already in this retailer, what is my best guess as to why? "Because they've never seen anything like this" is rarely the case.

- What is the buying structure at my targeted retailers? Who buys what? No two retailers are the same.

- Which retailers do I have in mind for this product, and why? "Because they have over 3,000 stores" is not a good answer!

- Do I understand which retailers are considered competition by the retailers I am targeting?

- What are the "reasons to be" for my products (see Chapter 10). What specific markets, needs/trends are being addressed?

- Am I prepared to offer this as an exclusive to a retailer? If not, who else will be seeing it?

- How will I facilitate orders (EDI capabilities, etc.)?

- Where is the shipping point for my product(s)?

- Where are they sourced?

- Do I have packaging capabilities?

- Can I execute pre-ticketing, special bar coding, and RFID requirements?

- Have my items been quality tested or will they stand up to third-party quality testing?

- Have I thoroughly shopped the stores of my targeted retailers and devised a unique game plan for each, which refers to their current products, brands, fixturing, and pricing?
- Have I refilled my Xanax prescription? Just joking!

This is a lot to consider, yet, as we always say in our seminars, "don't waste an audience." You will rarely get a second opportunity to present your products and your company to a given Pencil.

Pencil Point # 9

Don't attempt to meet with a Pencil until you are ready!

Chapter 4: Who Should I Target?

Start-up suppliers often make assumptions regarding where their product should be distributed based on factors that have no basis in retail reality. For example:

- Assuming that a product belongs in a high-end retailer because that is where the company principal shops and other venues are unfamiliar.

- Assuming that a product belongs in a mass retailer because it would mean a lot of business.

- Assuming that a product does *not* belong in a mass retailer because such a move would bastardize a brand.

- Assuming that a product belongs in a prestigious department or specialty store because the supplier wants prestige.

It is most important to remember that there are distinct differences between how specialty stores, department stores, mass retailers, and food and drug retailers operate. Beyond that, there are pricing, branding, and presentation standard differences within these groups that will point you in a direction based on the characteristics of your product and your ability to execute.

It is important to be honest with yourself regarding your ability to manage the challenges associated with various distribution tiers in order to benefit from the opportunities. If you are unable to execute the pricing, packaging, ticketing, and quantity requirements of a mass customer, for example, then you may need to revise your distribution plan (and your financial goals) to accommodate a specialty store launch. As of this writing, many transportation companies are creating niche businesses in third party logistics for smaller suppliers to include warehousing, ticketing, inventory management, and of course, transportation of goods.

One way to further refine your distribution strategy is to contact independent reps who manage your product category for the accounts you are targeting. Generally you can find reps who manage territories that will include geographically-designated specialty stores anchored by one or more major accounts. If the rep organization is a good fit for your company, is established in the category/product you are selling, has existing relationships with desirable retailers, and is interested in your product, this alone may drive your initial distribution strategy (if all of the execution elements are in place). We address this more in depth later in the book.

Logical Steps to Distribution

It used to be that suppliers launched products in the specialty tier, built that business, then moved on to larger distribution. This strategy allowed the supplier to work out the bugs on a more forgiving customer (specialty stores), fine-tune product sourcing and pricing, and then move more confidently into working with the big guys. Nowadays, with the emergence of mass retailing, even established suppliers can try to leapfrog over logical progression, right to where the volume is (with varying success).

If we had our "druthers," we would advise everyone, from pure start-ups seeking launch to established companies seeking new product distribution, to take the time to start small and move up the volume chain. Many established companies choose aggressive distribution over a logical progression and find out at the end of the day that they were not equipped to manage the business, or worse, that they are doing it at little or no profit.

Pencil Point # 10

Plan your product launch around a logical progression of distribution, or risk becoming a casualty (or a not-for-profit organization).

A Word on Licensing

We have spoken to many aspiring licensees (those who manufacture and sell certain products under a license), who misunderstand how licensing works. People tell us that they have developed a NASCAR™ corkscrew, or a major football team keychain. We hear from many people who say they want to "get into licensing. . ."

Those who aspire to become licensees for products need to know the following about major licensors (companies that own and manage a given license):

- They generally find licensees for products that they believe fit in with their image and goals (they go to suppliers rather than suppliers going to them — but there are exceptions).

- They seek out suppliers who have an established and demonstrated expertise in a given category or item.

- They seek out suppliers who have existing distribution in retail tiers that are compatible with their image and goals.

- They, like major retailers, are increasingly interested in expanding their current licensees' reach rather than bringing in new licensees (e.g., giving the sock licensee the license to make hats as well).

- No one can manufacture *as though* they are a licensee without being sanctioned by or entering into a contract with the main licensing body (well, you can, it's just called trademark and copyright infringement!).

- Licensors exercise varying amounts of control over their properties both in terms of what products will be licensed (you can't assume that NASCAR™ even *wants* a keychain in their line-up without asking first), and the design of those products.

In general, licensing is more of an established supplier growth strategy than a start-up launch strategy. Licensing is a complex business and many an established supplier has been burned by trying to guess what the next hot license will be, satisfying royalty minimums, and/or getting stuck with license-specific inventory that has no outlet.

Pencil Pearl

Carol was charged with selling a stable of hot and not-so-hot licensed products back in her sales days. At one point, she handled a major multi-character license that had withstood the test of time. A Pencil for what was considered at the time to be a large account (over 800 stores) looked at one of the just-sketched t-shirt screen prints and liked the looks of it. Carol put in the order, only to hear that the design had not yet been approved by the licensor (this was considered a mere technicality, since her company felt certain of their ability to execute approvable designs). The order went through and, three months later, the licensor rejected the design on the grounds that (the particular character) "wouldn't hold a baseball bat like that." There was no talking them out of it and everyone agreed the ruling was arbitrary, but that didn't keep the order from being cancelled; and Carol had to explain to her Pencil why she was allowed to buy an unapproved design. Talk about a credibility hit!

Pencil Point # 11

Licensing can be tremendously rewarding but is not an amateur endeavor.

Chapter 5: The Pencil Perspective and What It Means to Your Strategy

A typical Pencil's day is filled with multiple internal meetings, delegating to (and often training) assistants, checking sales, reacting to sales, following up on orders, rummaging through boxes of samples from numerous vendors, responding to e-mails from multiple internal and external sources, and scheduling and conducting meetings with a steady parade of vendors!

Being a Pencil is a TOUGH, complex, and often thankless job with long hours and the fact is, despite holding the buyer title, many buyers no longer *buy*. Buyers go to school or enter into training programs to buy product and yet, depending on the size of the retailer and department they go to work for, many go on to become *implementers* of corporate programs. That can make the job even more mundane and stressful, and for Pencils with a creative bent (which describes many who pursue this career), that's a real burn.

Therefore it is very important for vendors or aspiring vendors to constantly ask themselves three questions:

- How am I making my Pencil's job easier?
- What can I do to acknowledge that my Pencil is a buyer?
- Am I treating my Pencil as a partner or as an adversary?

The answers to all questions are covered extensively throughout the rest of the book. We are introducing them here to set the stage for a Pencil-centric *mindset* that should be in place from the first time you meet with any Pencil and throughout your business relationship.

Buyer and licensor Pencils rarely act autonomously and many of the demands they make on their vendors including packaging changes, price reductions, and style changes, have been handed down for them to implement. One of three misguided vendor reactions often follows:

- Taking demands *personally* and going on to hold grudges against the Pencil who delivered the challenge.
- Viewing such challenges as problems rather than *inevitable* aspects of doing business.
- Vowing "never to go to that much trouble again."

In short, vendors become so protective of their products and profitability, that they maintain a guarded and defensive position at all times without realizing it. Some even perpetuate this "us and them" attitude throughout their organizations. Pencils pick up on this and find those vendors to be tedious, uncooperative, and, in the end, replaceable!

Pencil Point # 12

Pencils have alternatives to replace defensive, argumentative, and uncooperative suppliers.

A "Partnership" Primer
(It's Not What You Might Think)

During an organizational assessment launch meeting with a successful apparel company, the company principal expressed a common sentiment, "They (Pencils), use the word 'partnership' a lot and 'vendor partner' when they aren't partners at all! They just squeeze and squeeze until we can't make any money!" The company principal was operating under a common false assumption, that "partnership" means that the Pencil is responsible for vendor profitability. The hard reality is that *vendors* are responsible for their own profitability and these days, for their Pencil's profitability as well. What? How unfair! Perhaps. Yet it is a reality nonetheless and one that vendors who want to stay in business must acknowledge in every decision they make.

Pencil Point # 13

Retailers are not responsible for your profitability!

Countless articles (and even college courses), are sprouting up regarding the "Wal-Mart effect" and the impact that Wal-Mart is having on the vendor community. We view the Wal-Mart effect as an incredible learning opportunity for any vendor doing business today. In our consulting work, we meet many supplier company principals who disagree with the state of things, or start-ups who vow not to sell to Wal-Mart. Neither point of view will change the fact that retailers around the world are emulating Wal-Mart's cost-cutting practices at every turn in order to become more efficient and profitable.

When planning for new or ongoing product and/or licensing placement with any major retailer, a vendor must know that there are no guarantees and that the retailer has *no* obligation to:

- Source product from any particular region or support vendors who do.
- Buy or keep buying from any particular vendor regardless of their position in the industry.
- Support any particular brand or license.
- Buy any product regardless of its features and attributes.
- Ensure vendor profitability.

With that in mind, vendors have two options:

- To work out their own product, licensing, and distribution strategies and mixes in such a way as to be profitable at the end of the day (not necessarily with every product and in every retailer).
- To just say "no" to certain retailers, licensing opportunities, and product categories.

So, what then is "partnership" for goodness sake?

Partnership is:

- Realizing at all times that the Pencil is your customer.
- Taking full responsibility for your own profitability.

- Taking full responsibility for your product and licensing choices.

- Planning inevitable financial allowances for your Pencils, including mark-down assistance, co-op advertising, slotting allowances (depending on the product), and returns.

- Making proactive infrastructure changes (rather than waiting until they become an emergency or a Pencil demand).

- Keeping pace with technological advances.

- Hiring and maintaining highly skilled and trained personnel (who may or may not be family members or friends).

- Doing everything you can to make your Pencil's job easier.

These may seem like daunting requirements, but retailing is not for the faint of heart! In our experience, partnership often begins as a one-way proposition and then ideally it evolves into:

- Key branding and licensing opportunities being realized.

- More face-time with your Pencils.

- Eligibility for expanded space and distribution.

- Minimization of punitive practices.

Pencil Point # 14

When suppliers do their part, they become partners with their Pencils.

Chapter 6: How to Pursue the Pencil

Start-ups usually have many questions about how to get a foot in the door, and we've yet to meet an established vendor who doesn't hope to expand into a new department within a store or gain new retail distribution.

Your Next Prospect Is … the Entire Store

We often tell our established supplier clients that their next best prospect is "the entire store." In other words, once you are doing business within a given department at a given retailer, the most logical next move is to try to get your products placed within other departments in the same store. To use a tired sales phrase, this is truly the low hanging fruit.

Start-up suppliers also need to be aware of this opportunity, since it can result in new business without the cost and effort associated with opening an entirely new account. One reason that some established vendors become paralyzed at the prospect of selling to a new department is because, these days, separate departments operate more like separate retailers than parts of the same company. In effect, you are cold calling on a retailer you are already selling. We actually think this presents tremendous advantages for a few reasons:

- You have the ability to start warm via Pencil referrals.
- You already understand that retailer's systems and procedures.
- You can easily parlay current successes into other departments (it is documented in their main system as proof, and your current Pencil can validate).

The trick is to know when another department is viewed as *competition* by your current Pencil and to manage the issue accordingly. Note that we said *manage*. No vendor should get stuck in a relationship or department-driven rut if their product offering supports expansion. Know that special or existing relationships didn't necessarily drive your competition's presence in more than one department; they took risks to make it happen.

Pencil Pearl

As an Account Executive for a major private label supplier, Carol was charged with placing everything from hair clips to lava lamps in a major mass retailer (the supplier's excellent sourcing led to quite a diverse product offering). Her existing relationship was with the women's accessories Pencil, and she had built a multi-million-dollar business within that department. The hot new item off the line was an inflatable furniture "room in a box" concept that could be offered at an unprecedented low retail after enjoying a successful run in department stores. Carol's first instinct was to think of some way to convince her women's accessories Pencil to try it. This was the stretch of all stretches for a Pencil whose profitability depended on hats, gloves, purses, and belts! The Pencil respectfully took a temporary pass, but after a bit of convincing on Carol's part, eventually agreed that she would test it if the furniture Pencil turned it down. The furniture Pencil said she didn't "see it in (her) department." The women's accessories Pencil, true to her promise and with a groan, made good on the test. That test sold 50% in the first week and in short order turned into a $5 million success. That was on *one item*!

At the retailer's yearly convention, the furniture buyer came by to say that the item absolutely belonged in her department (she had seen the sales figures)! Carol had to respectfully remind her that she had passed on it a few months prior.

This story illustrates how in-store competition can work to your advantage when attempting to get new items placed. It also calls attention to a common misperception: that retail buying structures are fine-tuned in such a way that every item has its place. In fact, as retail buying structures have grown, Pencils are charged with narrowing their focus, and "gray" items (those that fall between Pencil departments) are more common as a result.

Depending on who you are working with, they can be viewed as problems or opportunities.

While it is possible to get the same product placed in more than one department, in-store competition makes these opportunities riskier. Should you want to expand placement of the same items, always ask your current Pencil's permission to approach another department. If your Pencil says "no way," then don't do it unless you believe the pay-off is worth the destruction of your existing business and relationship with your current Pencil. Examples of this kind of multiple placement are:

- Hair accessories placed in the women's, children's, and HBA departments
- Children's car safety items placed in the infant and automotive departments
- Backpacks placed in the accessories and luggage departments
- Flashlights placed in the automotive and housewares departments

The real opportunity lies with placing and *creating* line extensions with other departments in mind. For example, if your core competency is women's hats, do any of the styles lend themselves to children's? Can you combine items together into gift packs and sell them to a gift Pencil?

You can begin the new item exploration any number of ways:

1. Ask your current Pencil for a referral

The conversation may go something like this:

"Marcie, do you know the buyer in the automotive area?"

"Yes, I think it's John Jones."

"We've expanded our line to include car safety items and we'd like to talk to him. If you have his contact number and e-mail address that would be great. Otherwise, we'll track it down. I would really appreciate it if you put in a good word for us if he mentions talking to me."

From there, your Pencil may volunteer an insight into the Pencil prospect, offer to make a call for you, or at the very least, provide a great reference for you.

More than once, Carol's Pencils responded with "Wait a minute ... Maybe I want a crack at these, they're great!"

2. Make a "cold call" leveraging current success

The conversation/message may go something like this:

"Hello, Mr. Jones. This is Carol Spieckerman with Fantastic Hats. We are a current supplier with you, vendor # 987654 (allows him to look up your performance). Marcie Abernathy in department 36 suggested I contact you to discuss our automotive safety line for kids. We are seeing Marcie this coming Thursday at 9:00, and would love to make plans to meet you any time after 11:00. If I don't hear from you, I'll follow up again when we're in your offices."

Then, confirm your call with an e-mail:

SUBJECT: VENDOR # 987654

Dear Mr. Jones:

I just left word for you regarding our automotive safety line for kids. We have developed quite a successful business with Marcie Abernathy in department 36 (our sales are up 30% year-to-date) and she suggested that I contact you for an appointment.

We will be seeing Marcie this coming Thursday at 9:00 and would welcome the opportunity to meet with you while we are in your offices (any time after 11:00).

Thank you for your consideration. I look forward to meeting you soon.

Best Regards, Carol Spieckerman

Whatever you do, be respectful and rather formal. No "Hey, John."

Be persistent and explore lots of options. As mentioned previously, many vendors make the mistake of assuming that major retailers have all categories worked out when in fact, many items (especially those that are trend-driven), may not have a logical place. It therefore behooves a supplier to "show it around" to increase the chances of a risk-taking Pencil seeing an out-of-the-box opportunity.

3. Leverage rejection

If one Pencil rejects an item as not being appropriate for their department, don't argue (unless you have a compelling reason or clear success that you can cite), ask him where he thinks it should go. If your Pencil says "...really, this is a great item but I think it belongs in gifts, not accessories." Your reply, "... interesting, who buys gifts?" From there, you can contact the new Pencil prospect saying, "John Jones in Department 63 really loved our item but suggested that I contact you to explore opportunities in Gift." Use any and all comments as leverage for new opportunities. Even negative remarks can provide leverage. If the same Pencil adds on, "... and really, I think it would be more viable if you added more colors," then add that to your prospecting call, "... John made some excellent color suggestions that we went ahead and sampled. I'd like to get your thoughts." This implies that, while the first Pencil didn't take the item, nevertheless it provoked interest and some kind of collaboration took place.

If your current Pencil becomes territorial in any way, again, you will need to either mitigate the issue (convince them that placement in another department will not compete with your current business), or proceed at your own risk!

If a Pencil referral is not an option, for whatever reason (and, as with any referral, only ask for one if you will get a good report), contact the prospect at regular (but not annoying), intervals, say ... every two weeks up to three times (or more frequently if you will be in their offices seeing other Pencils). Don't just use the same spiel every time. Keep it fresh.

4. Visit their department in the store and mention an insight

"Children's safety items are really catching on in automotive, and I was surprised not to see any in your department. As the leading provider of children's safety items, with a great business in Department 36, we can help you put together a program that will capitalize on this trend."

5. Keep abreast of Pencil personnel changes

"I spoke with John Jones a couple of times about the tremendous growth in children's safety items. Unfortunately, we never got it off the ground, yet the business has never been better. Knowing that you came from the children's department as his replacement, I think you'll understand the opportunity. . ."

6. Refer to success with a competing or non-competing retailer

(Be careful here!) "I wanted to speak with you about a program that has completely exceeded plan for 8 months running at Target. . ."

If you don't get anywhere after several reasonable attempts, back off! Whatever you do, don't bad-mouth the Pencil or whine to your other Pencils ("The jerk never called me back ..."). Put it on your calendar to follow up again at the next pre-season opportunity (when you are seeing your other Pencils to plan the next season). We can't tell you how many times certain products have just popped into consciousness after months of trying then letting it rest. Keep your cool, don't take it personally, don't over-communicate, give it a rest, and then follow up again.

Pencil Point # 15

"No" means "Not yet" more often than you'd think.

To Send or Not to Send . . . Samples!

One of the top questions we get from aspiring suppliers who have made some contact with Pencils is, "She told me to send samples and she would get back to me. Should I do that? What about knock-offs?"

Our general opinion here (although there are exceptions) is that every effort should be made to show your products in person. Not so much because of the threat of knock-offs, although there are retailers who have reputations for this, but because it simply offers a better presentation. Sending your samples to a Pencil is still a presentation, and if your products are dismissed out of hand because the Pencil was busy or had a bad day, there goes your first presentation, and the chances of getting another one go down exponentially from there.

To put it in perspective, in twenty years of working with established accounts, Carol received *one* response from blind samples sent to a Pencil. Again, there are exceptions. If your products fill an immediate need, i.e. a void left by another supplier, you may get a call back. But we still advocate pushing for an appointment.

If you are asked to send samples in advance, try to think of a respectful but compelling reason why an appointment is a better idea. For example, "I'll be out your way the week of August 13th with my product designer and sourcing manager ... truly, they are so knowledgeable about this category and this product, I think meeting them will make a real difference in your perspective on our product."

Pencil Point # 16

Getting an appointment should be your first goal. Send samples in advance only if all else fails.

A Word on Knock-Offs

One of the greatest fears expressed by start-up companies (and some established companies) is the fear of having their product duplicated by a sinister retailer or big time competitor. Anyone doing business today has to view knock-offs as *inevitable,* and that is why putting your life savings into a one-hit wonder product is so short-sighted. Unless you are ready to embark on the costly and time-consuming patenting process, obsessing on the potential for knock-offs misses the point entirely and reveals a lack of long-term planning. If a competitor or a retailer knocking off one of your products would sink your ship, you aren't ready to do business with major retailers. That is why every vendor must be thinking one step ahead. What is the next permutation of this product? How will I add features, lower prices, expand it into other items, update the colors, make it appropriate for other seasons, etc.?

The ability to constantly update, change and provide exemplary service are requirements for long-term success.

That is not to say that you don't use caution and restraint with product information and prototypes. We have met with otherwise reasonable people who, in their zeal to spread the word about their products, sent out costly blanket mailers of samples to anyone with an address! Some of those suppliers did indeed get their products knocked off and, since they had lost track of where the samples had been distributed, they had little recourse.

Pencil Point # 17

You can't hold your product samples so close that no one can see them, and you can't lose track of where they have gone. Fear of knock-offs will limit your options and can be a distraction from the real work that needs to be done.

How Else Can I Get an Appointment?

Probably the best way, as we touched on earlier, is what we call "I'll be out your way." A Pencil often doesn't want to have any obligation or imply any commitment by requesting that you come to their office or make a special trip. Therefore, if you want to make a presentation, call or send an e-mail saying, "I'll be out your way the week of September 19th and would welcome the opportunity to meet with you sometime that week at your convenience. I won't take more than 30 minutes of your time." "Out your way" keeps it loose, as does the week-long time frame (it allows them to work with several days and times). If they respond with, "Sorry, I'd love to meet with you but I'm on vacation that entire week," then respond that you may be able to arrange staying a bit longer or "shift" the days.

Back in Carol's sales days, this was surprisingly effective. Often the response was "Okay, how about Friday of that week at 7:00 a.m.? That's all I have and we'll have to keep it to the 30 minutes." Carol's response, "Terrific. I'll look forward to seeing you then and we'll have no problem keeping within that time limit." See the later chapter on meetings to take it from there (take special note of the comments about staying within the agreed time frame)!

Try taking it a step further by using that appointment as leverage to make another one at the same retailer, i.e., "I'm seeing John at 7:00 a.m. on Friday, the 21st. If you have any time that day, I would like to drop by." An existing appointment has the effect of making you look like an insider.

Pencil Point # 18

Getting Pencil appointments takes patience, determination, and the ability to leverage success ***and*** *rejection.*

Should I Play Ball with Gate-Keeping Tactics?

By "gate-keeping," we are referring to various ways that retailers will screen you before considering a meeting (the sample-in-advance request mentioned previously is an example). Larger retailers have established new-vendor procedures that involve filling out and submitting forms about your company and your products for consideration. There is no reason in the world not to play ball with the gate-keeping while you also attempt to reach Pencils directly. In fact, when you do speak to a Pencil, he or she will often ask if you are a vendor of record. You can respond that you are in the process (and they may offer to put you on the fast track if they like your products).

A couple of the major retailers also offer seminars that teach new vendors their processes and procedures. These seminars usually aren't cheap, but we say they are a good investment. Again, one of your greatest assets as a supplier will be the ability to understand your retailer's business (and talk their language). You are playing by the rules and doing your best to learn. Advertisements for these seminars appear in various trade publications.

Pencil Point # 19

Playing by the rules and supplementing your direct contact efforts will greatly increase your chances of gaining a Pencil's interest.

Chapter 7: Are <u>You</u> the Best "Face" for Your Product?

Entrepreneurs are understandably attached to their products and can therefore mistakenly assume that they are the best front person for any retail presentation.

We believe that if you do not possess a retail background (preferably, specific experience with the retailer you are targeting), you are probably doing yourself a disservice by insisting on presenting your own products. As noted before, knowledge of your product is important but it is only part of the equation. Few start-up company principals can expect to obtain the in-depth, retailer-specific knowledge required for a home run in the first meeting with a major Pencil. However, this doesn't mean that you shouldn't be present. We strongly encourage company principals to be present in these initial meetings. How else will you learn?

If Not Me, Then Who?

Barring hiring an in-house sales representative (which many start-ups find cost prohibitive), many independent sales representatives work on a commission basis. Every effort should be made to find one who possesses specific experience with the retailer you are targeting. Running ads in relevant trade publications or internet job sites should yield many qualified applicants at minimal cost.

In our consulting business, we are often called upon to recruit, interview, and hire personnel for our clients as part of an overall organizational strategy. What we find, time and time again, is that experience with specific classes of retail trade is much more relevant than category experience. Start-up and established companies often learn this the hard way after assuming the reverse. For example, if you are trying to get a line of bed sheets placed in Target, you would be better off hiring a sales rep who sold baby clothes to Target than hiring a rep who sold bed sheets to "mom and pop" specialty stores.

Major retailers in particular utilize very specific systems and, if a rep has maintained positive relationships with other Pencils in the store group, it should be easy to procure referrals to pertinent Pencils in other departments. Increasingly, major retailers want to work with suppliers who understand *their way of doing things.*

Pencil Pearl

We were on retainer with a consumer products company that had already hired a salesperson. They asked for our advice regarding the best compensation structure for her. After reading her résumé and hearing her demands to date, we suggested they consider replacing her immediately. She possessed no previous wholesale sales experience, no experience with major mass retailers (the class of trade they were targeting), and was demanding a cents-on-the-dollar commission arrangement that was completely out of line with industry standards. When we asked why they had become so focused on her in light of the facts, the sales manager replied, "You don't understand – she is *enchanted* with our product!" Carol had to tell him honestly that in 20 years of selling everything from children's apparel to cameras, she could not say she was "enchanted" with any of the products she had sold. In spite of this, she consistently grew businesses from zero to multi-millions. How? By being "enchanted" with knowing her Pencils' business, building relationships, and making money!

Pencil Point # 20

Don't let your personal attachment to your idea lead to foolish hiring decisions, and if you can't afford to support a professional, qualified sales effort (yourself or an outside party), you should reconsider your venture.

Bringing in Help
Independent versus In-House Sales Representation

Consider sales and distribution strategies to be yet another area where the dominance of mass retailers has changed the rules. As the sales volume potential and the complexity of retail have increased, so has the need for control of the sales process on the part of suppliers.

While there are still independent reps fortunate enough to enjoy major mass store business, most of those accounts have long since been brought in-house by supplier companies. As supplier companies became aware of the sometimes staggering commission pay-outs for spotty sales results in their higher-volume businesses, bigger accounts were slowly brought back into the home office. Few supplier companies trust a Wal-Mart or Target account to an independent sales representative (there are exceptions); yet well-chosen independent reps can provide tremendous access, retailer-specific understanding, and cost savings for supplier companies seeking wide distribution. We find that most of the independent reps who currently call on major retailers are still there for a reason – they are doing a better job than their supplier companies could do with in-house representation for those same accounts!

The following outlines some of the characteristics, advantages and disadvantages of working with independent and direct reps.

Independent Reps:

Contract employees who represent your company's products and others

Best Suited to:

- Territory specialty store sales
- Instant access without overhead for start-up ventures
- Targeted accounts where access would otherwise prove elusive

Advantages:

- Paid on performance
- No overhead expenses
- Existing access and knowledge
- Ability to cover territory
- Open-ended relationship with little obligation
- Specialize in selling to specific customers or markets
- Can offer systems and solutions that increase Pencil profitability (since they are paid more as business increases)
- Less turn-over

Disadvantages:

- Primary loyalty to retailer, not to supplier
- Possible product conflicts (disclosed or not)
- Lack of full commitment and comprehensive product knowledge for a given supplier that they represent
- Lack of oversight
- Complexity of accountability
- Strategies for sharing in punitive retailer practices and developing commission structure can be daunting
- Lack of cohesive culture and execution of consistent corporate message and standards

In-House/Direct Reps

Employees of your company who are on your payroll and earn a salary, commission, or combination of both.

Best Suited to:

- High-maintenance major accounts where being in the "home office" presents a distinct advantage in terms of support and oversight
- Well-funded companies who can afford the overhead and who seek consistent effort with oversight

Advantages:

- Committed to supplier success and mitigation of retailer conflicts
- Primary loyalty to supplier, not retailer
- In-depth and ongoing product knowledge and training
- Complete oversight
- "Home office" support and immediate access

Disadvantages:

- Refining and updating salary and bonus structure in relation to volume achieved/retention can be daunting
- Overhead expenses (travel, insurance, savings plans, etc.)
- Close-ended relationship with more potential for litigation

For start-up supplier companies, sales representation choices are a question of access vs. control. Regardless of the strategy or combination of strategies that you choose to pursue, choose your front person wisely. This is not the place to cut corners by hiring a friend, family member, or personality salespeople touting dubious "connections."

Pencil Point # 21

Your Pencil prospects want to work with people who understand their business. Do whatever is necessary to find those people.

Using the Right Hiring Standards for Your Sales Organization

Hiring sales personnel based on personality or connections is short-sighted since these days, Pencils are likely to be frequently rotated throughout a given retailer or within a licensor's various departments. In the old days, a given Pencil could stay in the same position as long as ten or fifteen years.

Hiring staff is a significant *investment*, especially for a small to medium sized company. Often we are called into companies to fix employee problems that could have been avoided altogether had higher standards and better hiring practices been in place. These include:

- Employees who are understood to be unsuitable for certain Pencil presentations (too volatile, take things personally, argumentative, bad appearance, don't listen).
- Employees who are generating sub-standard work yet they are the only ones who "do what they do."
- Employees who have to be worked around because of personality problems or lack of cooperation.
- Employees who are holding a company hostage with threats (implied or feared) of discriminatory lawsuits.

Supplier company principals often operate under an assumption that the product sells itself. We have yet to find a product that sold itself, but we'll keep looking. What we *have* found are supplier company principals who have so much of their identity wrapped up in the product offering that they downplay the relevance of anything not related to product itself (sales representation in particular).

Many principals and managers of supplier companies tell us honestly that they don't *know* what standards to use in hiring anymore and they feel intimidated by the increased expectations of their biggest Pencils. Our extensive survey work with top Pencils confirms that they notice and care about leadership, capability, communication, and professionalism within their supplier companies more than one would imagine. The process of hiring the right people should be given careful consideration for this reason.

Attracting Talent

Established supplier companies have the advantage of being just that, established. As such, they are able to attract, pick, and choose sales help rather easily. Start-up companies find themselves in the position of having to sell their products and their company to qualified sales people.

Many start-ups don't see it that way (see the Pencil Pearl earlier in this chapter). Their standards for sales representation can be what we call "cheap and cheerful." That is, hiring people as inexpensively as possible who have enthusiasm and zeal for the company's product is the top criterion. Retail is far too complex and specialized for start-up companies and the stakes are way too high for established suppliers to take sales risks. To put it bluntly, an inexperienced salesperson, even working in tandem with an enthusiastic entrepreneur, is not the best choice for today's big Pencils. Furthermore, taking such a risk may permanently close your prospect's door.

We coach our start-up and established clients to swallow their egos and be willing to take an occasional back seat to those who know. Talented sales representation can be your start-up venture's biggest asset. You owe it to yourself to remember the following:

- Your biggest Pencils want to work with *professionals* who communicate well, have positive personalities, and know their business. Hire accordingly!

- Positive hiring experiences go a long way in creating positive employees and your Pencils will notice as well.

- Hiring personnel who consistently raise the bar in your organization, rather than maintaining the status quo, will create a dynamic impression of your organization for your most valued Pencils.

- Well-placed independent sales reps become part of your company's brain trust and can increase your retail and product knowledge exponentially in a short amount of time.

With all of this in mind, your initial pitch will actually be to the talented, connected sales people that you, or an outside consultant, brought to your company.

Five questions to ask yourself before approaching a sales representative:

1. What is my market niche (refined through market research, as mentioned earlier)?

2. What are my product's advantages and disadvantages?

3. Which channels of distribution have I targeted for my product, and why?

4. Which specific retailers?

5. What commission and/or salary arrangements am I comfortable with?

All of the questions are answered in newmarketbuilders' "Are You Really Ready for Retailers?" checklist (Chapter Three).

Pencil Point # 22

As a start-up, your first sell will be to top-notch sales representation. Swallow your ego and be willing to learn from those who know.

Chapter 8: Pencil Presentation Preliminaries

You worked hard to get this far, now the real work begins! The fact that Pencil meetings are shorter in duration than ever before also makes them more stressful. Reacting to these constraints by attempting to force more content into a shorter time frame will only lead to frustration and disappointment.

Most vendor companies, especially start-ups, go into meetings excited about their products. After all, a lot of work went into checking the trends, sourcing, making samples, and determining strategic price points. While showing product may very well be *one* of the goals of a meeting, it should never be the *only* goal.

All meetings should be viewed as multi-faceted opportunities to demonstrate the preparedness, professionalism, and proactive approach of your company (the "Three P's" of Pencil meetings, if you will). Additionally, remaining open and listening are important since Pencil meetings always offer an invaluable and ongoing crash course in retail.

Pencils are pressed for time and expect a strategically-edited, logically grouped presentation. When your Pencil is giving you an hour, exactly one hour, to greet, introduce your company, and show product, you need to work from a plan. In this section, we address preparation, execution, and follow-up techniques that will ensure the most efficient use of the time allotted.

Develop a Plan of Action

The number one complaint we hear from vendor companies is, "Retailers never give us enough time ..." and, predictably, the number one complaint we hear from Pencils is "Vendors are disorganized, and they don't plan." Many Pencil meetings end with the vendor saying, "Wait, we didn't even talk about. . ." and the Pencil fuming because the meeting ran over with no respect for their time. That's a terrible note on which to end your meeting (or begin a relationship)!

Pencil Point # 23

Working from a meeting plan makes the best use of time and increases the perception of your company's competence.

Consider the following when planning your meeting:

Who will attend the meeting?

Many vendor companies have heard their Pencils begin a meeting with the comment "too many bodies in the room," yet they continue to fill the room on subsequent visits. Try to choose the people most effective and helpful to the Pencil, without respect to politics, position, or ego. That can be a tall order in some companies, but it is the only way to look at it if your goal is to conduct a Pencil-centric meeting.

That means:

- The president of the company doesn't necessarily go to every meeting (or conversely, doesn't sit all of them out).
- Product people are not an automatic presence (or conversely, may add value).
- Analytical staff may be an appropriate and welcome addition (or overkill).

The rule of thumb should be: Anyone without a speaking part and who does not add value to the meeting, should not attend. Also it should go without saying that anyone who is incapable of following the agenda, or anyone who is a loose cannon, is argumentative or is defensive, should not be invited.

Unfortunately, owners and top executives have been known to fall within these categories!

While we believe that well-trained salespeople should be able to handle most Pencil meetings, there are meetings that may require an additional presence:

- Those which will involve a more technical discussion e.g. thread counts, fabric weights, chemical compositions, or processes.
- Those which involve in-depth discussions of product and packaging development capabilities e.g. meetings with brand managers and/or licensors.

Pencil Pearl

One of our clients is a successful, multi-million-dollar, privately-held company which had recently lost two major programs to a competitor. The supplier company principal was feeling beaten up by her Pencils and didn't know how to stop the negative momentum. We surveyed their top retail and licensing Pencils in order to determine where break-downs were occurring. We were told repeatedly that our client was an unwelcome presence in meetings due to her argumentative nature and defensiveness about her pricing and products. Every meeting became tedious to the point of complete frustration. One Pencil remarked, "She doesn't seem to think that we have alternatives ...We do, and we are getting ready to look at them!" We conducted a Pencil Perception seminar for our client's entire organization, covering meeting procedure, conflict resolution, and effective follow-up. Many of the participants were relieved to have a structure underpinning what had always been a chaotic and nerve-racking process within the company. At our six month check-up, every Pencil commented on the improved communication with our client and one remarked that a "sea change" had taken place in the supplier company.

Rehearse

So few companies do this, and it is why most meetings run over and are disorganized. You haven't come this far to just wing it.

Without planning and setting agendas, meetings *will* meander, product will be left un-shown, and topics left un-discussed.

At least several days prior to a meeting, all parties attending the Pencil meeting should meet to review product, discuss problems and opportunities, and review the agenda. If a Power Point or similar presentation will be utilized, all parties (that includes top management), should walk through it noting their speaking parts and time allocation.

If you are using independent representatives who are based outside of your home office, every effort should be made to meet with the rep in advance of the Pencil meeting to review product and pricing and to discuss any new developments with the account. This is especially important for a first meeting with a Pencil and any time or money invested will be worth it.

Supplier companies often assume that sending disjointed sample presentations and printed information one or two days prior to a Pencil meeting is adequate to familiarize the rep with their product. Unfortunately, some reps encourage this practice by saying, "Just send the presentation to me and I'll figure it out." Supplier companies are happy to oblige in order to save time and additional travel expense. Much better for everyone to meet the day before to review the agenda, samples, pricing, and Pencil updates. The supplier sales managers in our coaching program who have taken this advice (always flying in a day early), consistently comment on the improvement in meeting outcomes and on the closer relationships they enjoy with their reps over time.

One person (we suggest the salesperson), should be in charge of keeping the time and ensuring that the meeting moves according to plan. Everyone should work through the agenda with the intention of sticking to their agreed place (and time allocation) regardless of their position in the company.

Deciding that the meeting will have to be about product only is unrealistic, since other topics invariably intervene. When companies rehearse meetings, they often discover their goals for the meeting were completely unrealistic given the time parameters of the Pencil. Blaming it on the Pencil's tight schedule is not an option. It is up to the vendor to conduct the most balanced, informative, and helpful presentation *within* the time given.

Pencil Point # 24

You didn't come this far to take shortcuts in your preparation!

Leave Room for Product Development

Many vendor companies prepare product for meetings under one of the following false, extreme assumptions:

- The Pencil is going to change everything anyway so we'll just show basic concepts and leave everything very open pending the Pencil's feedback.

■ We have worked so hard to make this product *perfect*. Lead times are too short for any changes and we are counting on not having to make any.

The first assumption may have your Pencil thinking that it would be easier to just give those orders directly to China. The second assumption will create tremendous tension for everyone and is unrealistic.

Today's suppliers must strike a balance between creating products and packaging in a complete vacuum (without retailer input), and walking into major retailers as an open book (with no particular point of view).

In general, in order to be successful, you must allow for a buy-in and participation from the retailer. Suppliers often develop product, packaging, and pricing under the assumption that they are striving for a perfect ideal and then convincing the retailer of the viability of that ideal. A more successful approach is to engage the retailer and remain as flexible as possible (with regard to packaging, pricing, and timing), for as long as possible while still maintaining a clear understanding of your "reason to be" and keeping your Pencil apprised of looming deadlines.

In other words, come to the meeting knowing what your product is *and what it isn't* for that specific retailer (one size does not fit all), based on market research and store visits. Be aware of that specific retailer's fixturing, pricing, and brand structure and come prepared to demonstrate how your product fits into that structure or fills a void. The most successful presentations are unique to each retailer and focus on their needs and requirements, as well as the attributes of the product being presented.

Pencil Point # 25

Involve your Pencil in the product development process while remaining mindful of your product's "reason to be."

How Much Do We Develop?

How much should you develop before coming to the retailer? The answer is "as much as you are willing to change!" Your optimal Pencil presentation will contain a fully developed plan-o-gram that refers to the retailer's fixturing (but is filled with your product). This presentation would be shown on storyboards with prototype sample supplementation and suggested pricing. You'll demonstrate an understanding of how their store looks and how your product *could* look in their store. Thus *begins* the conversation.

Never go into a meeting with a retailer with the goal of convincing them to buy what you have *as is*. Go in with the intention of beginning a dialog about your highly viable product and what you are able or not able to achieve in terms of product, packaging, and pricing changes, deliveries, quantities, and special requests.

We have worked with many supplier companies that continue to enjoy success and growth based solely on their ability to execute special requests and turn those requests on a dime.

Pencil Point # 26

Flexibility is the most important supplier quality in today's competitive environment.

Timing Is Everything

We often are asked, "When should we go?" All Pencils work within major buying and planning seasons that vary according to the products they buy. It used to be that if you missed the planning time for one of those seasons, you would need to wait for the next one (often up to six months later) if you hoped to get your product placed. It is still preferable to work with a Pencil at the beginning of their seasonal planning time, when they are previewing lines from their top suppliers and planning major buys. That said, we tell our clients that, while there are *advantageous* times to show product, the only truly bad time is when the Pencil isn't in the mood to see you!

Chapter 9: Building a Pencil-Friendly Presentation

As stated before, the most important thing to remember about product presentations in today's world is that they are the beginning of the sales process and not the end. That means that you will have to be ready and willing to change product and packaging that took you months to perfect, and you will have to be comfortable with presenting product one day, submitting samples the next, and receiving commitments sometimes weeks or months later.

Assuming you have already conducted market research and developed your reason to be, you should take the following steps to wrap up your pre-meeting preparations:

Conduct Pencil Research

Suppliers often maintain a myopic understanding of their Pencil's business. They become so focused on their product that they completely ignore overall store, licensing, or industry processes. Before your meeting, visit the Pencil company's web site and read any press releases, financial statements, investor reports, and note brand focus observations; read any and all trade publications that may have piled up on your desk; and check out the *Wall Street Journal, Fortune,* and *Business Week.* The goal is to become informed about the big-picture, including:

- Storewide branding initiatives including brand acquisitions and private labels (even if they don't seem to affect the departments you are targeting)
- Overall retail and licensing acquisitions, mergers, and program launches within the industry
- Pertinent demographic trends (ones that affect your business)
- News that affects your Pencil's other departments of responsibility (ones that may drive their business yet do not include your product)
- Top management changes within the Pencil's organization
- Technological or supply chain updates affecting the industry and/or your Pencil

Remember, your Pencils are probably responsible for more than just the category that covers your product; and they read the company newsletter and attend planning meetings. Therefore they are usually quite knowledgeable by osmosis. It is easy to spot a myopic supplier company (and they are far less interesting to work with).

Organize and Avoid Product Purge

The best-laid meeting plans can be completely derailed by a disorganized sample presentation.

We advocate grouping samples in some logical way and bagging, twist-tying, or boxing them together (whatever makes sense for your products), in those groupings prior to presentation. Doing so will help you bring product out in a logical presentation sequence rather than showing everything at once and overwhelming the Pencil (*product purge*). Pencils tell us that disorganized supplier presentations are a top frustration.

Pencil Pearl

One supplier we knew invited their junior product development person to every Pencil meeting. The company utilized independent sales representatives, and the product development person would fly out and meet the reps at various Pencil offices. Since she had a hand in designing most of the items in her category, she made it a point to bring every single piece, regardless of its relevance to the Pencil. She began each meeting either by dumping (literally), every piece out of the box and onto the table in front of the Pencil, or pulling random samples out of the box until all had found their way to the table (or the floor, or any surface that would hold them). The product development person said that the Pencils didn't mind her presentation "method." When we surveyed the client company's Pencils, they remarked that the *company* (not the product development person), was disorganized and "threw product up just to see what would 'stick' … they don't do their homework or they would know that 50% of what they are showing isn't right for my business."

Pencil Point # 27

Disorganized product presentations reflect poorly on your entire company, not just on the person conducting the presentation.

Mind the Details

If you are going to take the time to present a plan-o-gram or CAD representation of an "ideal" product placement, take the extra step of knowing and referencing their fixture dimensions and *fixture-fill* (the number of units that will fill a given fixture) as relates to your product. To present product that won't fit on your Pencil's fixture is, at the very least, unhelpful and shortsighted. Go out into the stores, measure the fixtures, purchase shelves and/or pegs of the same size, and work it all out *before* going into the meeting. The same goes for floor-ready product presentations ("PDQ's") and the like. This is especially important for start-ups or new product launches.

Pencil Point # 28

Don't hesitate to make investments in art, photos, computer-generated plan-o-grams and other presentation aids. Many companies use these

tools as a matter of course (and they may well be your competition)!

Dress to Impress

We hate it that we even have to cover this topic, but in our consulting work we continue to see too many problems regarding dress to ignore it.

Pencil dress has undoubtedly moved more toward casual. Unfortunately, the vendor community has taken this as a signal to respond accordingly (and often, to the extreme). We believe firmly that this is a mistake and that you should *always* dress professionally for a sales appointment.

Why?

- Even if your Pencil's organization encourages casual dress, you are not an employee in their organization.
- It demonstrates that something special is going on (and something is).
- Professionalism increases your negotiating leverage.
- Dressing professionally sends the proper message to outsiders about you and your organization.
- It shows respect for your Pencil.

Pencil Pearl

As a sales manager, Carol heard salespeople say more than once "They don't *pay* me enough to dress up." Her lack of tolerance for this attitude can be traced back to her first job in the apparel industry (over 20 years ago), as a showroom manager for a major children's wear company at the Dallas Apparel Mart. Carol owned one nice item, a reversible skirt, which she dutifully donned for her job interview along with hose, pumps, and one of a few decent blouses she owned (as was the uniform for ladies in those days)! After sailing through the interview, Carol's future boss asked a few questions, the last of which was "... and, uh ... can you look like *that* every day?" pointing to her outfit. She nervously assured him that she could and went on to turn that skirt inside out for an entire week until she mercifully received her first paycheck. That meager check went right to the discount store career section where a few more skirts and blouses were purchased. Needless to say, Carol's current career wardrobe does not include a single reversible skirt!

Dressing professionally for men doesn't have to mean a suit and tie (although there's certainly nothing wrong with that), but at least wear a sport coat, long-sleeved dress shirt, slacks, and a sturdy pair of high-quality, polished, leather shoes.

For women, we don't advocate getting any more casual than a nice sweater with slacks.

The only exceptions are if you are presenting a super-trendy, hip, fashion product to a retailer with a similar image. Even then, we still believe that more conservative options should be chosen when visiting a Pencil's corporate office.

These days, it is very difficult to convince vendors of the importance of professional dress and setting standards rather than mirroring off of others. We can only tell you that in years of working on both sides of the table and in numerous candid conversations with Pencils, dress does matter, it is noticed, and, when thoughtfully executed, it is appreciated and respected.

Pencil Point # 29

Regardless of your usual standards, those of your Pencil's office, and even "casual Friday," keep an edge by strengthening your resolve to dress professionally!

Show Respect

On your way to the meeting (or in the meeting itself), you will encounter various Pencil personnel, from the person at the front desk or lobby, to an assistant, to other Pencils you may happen upon. All should be greeted (unless otherwise engaged) and afforded the same courtesy and respect as your primary Pencil.

Pencil Point # 30

Never treat anyone in the Pencil organization as a means to an end.

Setting Up

When a buyer's assistant or buyer rescues you from the lobby, or when your company is called up, you are then ushered into your designated conference or sample room. At this time, your Pencil will usually say, "I'll give you a few minutes to set up." We are continually surprised by the number of companies who use this time to chat or check their voice mail. Set-up time should be used for just that — *setting up* — which should include the following:

Straighten - If there are other samples, paperwork, empty cups, etc. on the work surface or presentation screen, the best thing to do is ask if you may move them before your Pencil escort leaves the room. Regardless of how messy the room may look, whoever got it that way probably had a method to their madness. A messy room does not give you *carte blanche* to push piles onto the floor, make bigger piles, or completely clear a showing screen. We suggest asking permission to move items then neatly moving things over a bit or, with piles of stacked paper or reports, placing them neatly in the same order under the table or on the floor.

Work Within the Space - If you are wheeling four rolling cases into a 6' x 6' room, obviously something will have to go. Only take out what will reasonably fit within the space given. Any remaining cases or samples should be placed neatly out in the hall for easy retrieval or in some other vacant space that will not create an obstacle course for you or your Pencil.

Make Room For the Pencil - Set aside a space for your Pencil (with a chair) that allows room for his paperwork and a writing surface, and which offers the best view of your product.

Arrange Samples Logically - What you place out on the table or on the showing screen depends largely on your agenda and the size and type of your product. You may want to place the first group out and leave the rest aside initially. Product is distracting and, assuming the first few minutes of your meeting will be taken up with introduction, we tend to err on the side of "less is more." Exceptions come into play if your product is large, cumbersome, or difficult to retrieve or, conversely, very small, intricate, and time-consuming to arrange. Use good judgment and keep the following in mind.

- Arrange samples neatly, attractively, and in a logical, progressive order that follows the agenda.
- Any hidden or reserve samples should already be in a logical order from your pre-meeting packing back at the home office. You should have a mental picture of how those samples will be brought out throughout the meeting.

Tighten up Your Supporting Materials - All supporting materials, including agendas, presentation books, calendars, photographs, swatches, CAD drawings etc., should take up as little room as possible and be in logical order for quick retrieval. All Pencil materials should be placed neatly on the table, facing the Pencil space.

Pencil Point # 31

The more organized you are before your Pencil walks in, the more time you will have to show your products.

Compile

Compile all presentation materials in a Pencil-friendly format. How many times have we seen gigantic three-ring binders with combinations of photos, swatches, and art falling out, separate packets reflecting style numbers and pricing, all supplemented with spotty sample presentations? Put it all together in the neatest, clearest, most accurate one-stop-shop format you can possibly create!

Keep in mind the reality that final decisions are rarely, if ever, made at the point of presentation anymore. What are you leaving behind that will make it easy for the Pencil to recall and write when that time comes (sometimes weeks/months later)?

Pencil Point # 32

By the time line review rolls around, it should be easy for a Pencil to recall and write, based on your initial presentation and the materials you left behind.

Chapter 10: The Meeting

The room is set up, everything's in order. Your Pencil walks in. The meeting begins!

In-person meetings are coveted for good reason. They are the best opportunity to showcase your expertise, your professionalism, and the attributes of your products. It is also your best opportunity to *listen* and *learn* about your Pencil's needs and respond in a way that uniquely addresses them. That opportunity is forfeited, however, if the vendor's single-minded goal is to regain the opportunity to talk and to present.

Pencil meetings are a balancing act between staying on point and remaining receptive to what the Pencil is saying.

The Greeting

It should go without saying that, when a Pencil asks, "How are you doing?" the only acceptable answer is, "Terrific, and you?" The Pencil does not need to hear about your plane ride from hell, lost luggage, trouble getting to their facility, or flu-like symptoms. Keep it light and positive and don't waste time — the clock is ticking.

The number one greeting used with Pencils is some variation of "How's business?" This dreaded, inane cliché question should be avoided at all costs (simply because it **is** dreaded, inane and cliché). Better to mine all of the information that you stocked up on prior to the meeting for a pointed and insightful opening, which might include:

- *An Insight Regarding the Pencil's Business* - "Opening 60 stores in one quarter is a new record. Will there be any problem getting product to all of them in time?" Every now and then, a question like this reveals a need for product that's ready to ship. It also can spark a few comments about competitors who aren't delivering.

- *An Insight Into Overall Store Initiatives* - "That multimillion-dollar deal with Acme Licensing is unprecedented. Will you be implementing their brands in your departments as well?" This might open up all kinds of great information regarding future branding initiatives that you may or may not have been privy to otherwise.

Pencil Point # 33

The greeting is your first opportunity to demonstrate that you've done your homework.

Elevator Speeches for Everyone

When working with a new Pencil, rehearse and deliver an "elevator speech" about you, your company, and your products. Deliver it after the greeting.

- *When working with a completely new prospect:* "Fantastic Hats is the largest maker of women's and children's hats and the third largest maker of gloves. We've been in business since 1975 and I've been working for the company as a Senior Account Executive since 2000."

- *As a start-up:* "Fantastic Hats is a company I started after realizing that most children's hat styles are just adult styles made smaller. I focus completely on the children's market, at prices 20% below the competition in comparable fabrics, and with all styles as part of a coordinating accessories collection."

- *When working with a Pencil who has replaced another Pencil:* "Fantastic Hats is the largest maker of women's and children's hats and the third largest maker of gloves. We've been in business since 1975 and I've been working for the company as a Senior Account Executive since 2000. Over the past two years working with your predecessor, we grew the business from $500,000 to over $1.5 million at retail in Department 35 to become your second largest vendor."

It is surprising how many established companies forget that a new Pencil may not have any idea who they are and what they do! Additional pointers to keep in mind:

- Focus more than ever on making their job easier.
- For a start-up company, follow the advice in the chapters covering meetings regarding well-prepared handouts, information about the company, style sheets, etc.

■ For an established company working with a new Pencil, bring clearly formatted history of the business to-date, samples or pictures of currently booked styles, and a short list of any subjects that might need to be addressed.

As a start-up, your Pencil may interrupt you and say, "Really, the only thing I *might* be interested in are those fleece hats in purple." That is your cue to show the fleece hats in purple! Don't get caught up in forcing a long presentation if a prospect expresses a specific need. The quicker you accommodate that request, the more likely that Pencil will be to consider additional products later in the meeting.

Pencil Point # 34

Tell the Pencil who you are and why you are there.

Presenting Your Product's "Reason to Be"

In addition to following the logical order of sample presentation outlined previously, your presentation should focus on your product's reason for being, based on the research you have conducted up to this point including how it:

■ Fills a product void in the Pencil's assortment

■ Offers a price advantage

■ Offers a quality advantage at a great price

■ Is feature-rich at a great price

■ Is an update to an item that is selling well

■ Addresses a key trend

- Offers any of the advantages above vs. the competition
- Sold well in other venues (be careful here and be sensitive to competitive situations. It is wiser to say "Specialty stores were very successful with this style …" than "Off-price Bizarre bought tons of this.")

Don't waste the Pencil's time with product that does not have a clear reason for being, and be prepared to move on if your Pencil is clearly not interested in an item. The initial goal is to get through the full presentation. We find that a Pencil will often *provide* context for you later in a meeting that will give an opening to re-show an item (she may object to an item's bright color, giving you an opportunity to bring out a similar item shown earlier that was in a more subdued color). The point is not to counter every single objection, for several reasons:

- You will drag the meeting out needlessly, jeopardizing your chances of completing the presentation.
- You will wear your Pencil out and possibly create ill will.
- Any victory that you force at the table will almost certainly become a loss at line review. Again, your Pencil is not making decisions on the spot and he or she will remember the items that were forced and take them out at line review.

Pick your spots and if you truly believe that an item is a *miss*, validate your Pencil's concerns and make your case: "Marcie, that's exactly what we thought until we did the research — we were as surprised as anyone that customers prefer orange …"

Pencil Point # 35

Always strive to keep the Pencil meeting moving forward.

Objections Are Opportunities

If you are *prepared*, objections become *opportunities* to demonstrate features and discuss advantages; however, if every item becomes a defensive struggle, you will quickly lose credibility. Most Pencils *want* to learn, and appreciate well-taken points and additional information that will inform their decisions. *All* Pencils dislike argumentative, defensive, and tedious sales presentations.

Also keep the following in mind:

- Back up your claims with research in a respectful manner: "Market share for this product is growing at 20% per year vs. a category average of 3%."

- Pick up on signals throughout the meeting. Is your Pencil listening to you? Looking at his watch? If you believe you are making good time yet your Pencil seems frustrated or rushed, it's better to ask than to proceed as usual. Ask, "You seem to be in a bit of a rush yet we're still within the hour. Is everything okay?" Your Pencil may respond with, "We're spending too much time on this group. I really am not interested and would like to move on."

- Stay on point and on message but also read clues to move along. Don't blame your Pencil for being impatient. It is up to you to remain interesting and interested, and to present new insights and new product that will hold your Pencil's attention.

- Always end each agenda point with a recap of any agreements, courses of action, and follow-up. Then ask, "Do you have any questions?"

- Take notes. Assuming you will remember everything is a mistake — you won't. Taking notes also demonstrates interest and provides valuable information to take back with you.

- Don't be afraid to ask questions. If your Pencil runs through something rapidly or states something important too quickly for you to catch, back up and ask, "Marcie, do you mind repeating that, I'd like to write it down?" Or say, "Honestly I don't understand what you just told me. Do you mind running through it once more?" Trust your instincts. If you didn't get it, it probably bears repeating. If your Pencil uses inside terminology, don't hesitate to ask ("You've referred to 'initiative 83' several times, can you tell me what that is exactly?"). Then by all means, adopt the lingo from that point on. Practice saying, "I don't know but will you tell me?" and, "Please repeat that, I'd like to write it down."

- Remember the myth of "closing the sale." Your primary goal should be to "create a memory" by leaving easy-to-check photos, descriptions, pricing, and samples behind (not insisting on constant agreement or wasting valuable meeting time forcing product that will later be eliminated at line review)! Your Pencil should be able to pull out a file two months after your presentation and recall and write with ease.

■ Don't be afraid to ask for the *next* meeting. Some Pencils plan their schedules months in advance, and it isn't out of the question to schedule a follow-up meeting or a day for the next presentation.

Secret of Survival ... Strive for Correction

Many established and start-up suppliers are so worried about looking stupid or getting something wrong that they spend an inordinate amount of energy trying to cover their tracks, argue points, or back-track during Pencil meetings.

Although it may seem counterintuitive, we believe that vendors should occasionally strive for correction in order to keep the balance in a meeting and in order to learn more.

Let's be honest, Pencils like to correct vendors. You would be amazed at how a couple of corrections or clarifications can take the air out of a tense meeting and give you valuable information you would otherwise never have known.

Have you ever become annoyed by politicians or interviewers who are so on message that they don't seem to be listening to what is being said or asked? They continually move on to their next diatribe to ensure that they get it all in. Trust us, this is more annoying in a sales situation. Pencils, like everyone, want to be heard.

Pencil Point # 36

Being corrected can be the best thing that ever happened in a meeting. Don't waste energy trying to always be right or attempting to monopolize the dialog.

Chapter 11: The Final Wrap-Up and What to Avoid

You should always conduct some kind of wrap-up for your meeting for many reasons:

- You are showing once again that you were listening.
- You are demonstrating your intention of following up and taking care of your Pencil's concerns.
- You are re-stating any agreements made.
- You are providing an opportunity for your Pencil to add to the list if something was missed, or to correct any inaccurate assumptions.
- It provides an opportunity to re-state the *positive* aspects of the meeting.
- It provides an opportunity to re-state deadlines – yours and theirs.

A sample wrap-up conversation might go something like this:

"This has been a great meeting. I'm so glad you like the way we executed that group for you and your insights about getting an early read in the October new stores really make sense. To wrap this up, Marcie, I'm going to get back to you tomorrow on the best date we can hit on 10,000 units of style number 34987, we're going to add blue and green options to style 35876, and I'll expedite samples of those options to you a week before your line review. Finally, as we discussed, I'll need to have your commitments by next Friday at the latest in order to hit your start ship date. I'll look forward to meeting with you again on June 14th at 2:30 to go over the styles you chose in your June 7th line review. Did I leave anything out?"

To which your Pencil might reply:

"On second thought, I really need to have those samples sooner ... they'll need to be photographed before line review. Also, go ahead and make it 15,000 units on 34987."

Make your notes then leave with eye contact, a handshake, and a "Thank you!"

Remember that, from this point forward, much of your contact with your Pencil may be spotty e-mails and phone messages.

Pencil Point # 37

The end of your Pencil meeting is the time to ensure that you are moving in the right direction from that point forward.

If you plan on lingering in that space for any amount of time, ask permission! "It's going to take a few minutes to load up these samples, is the room booked?" or "Would it be possible for me to stay in here for a few minutes and make a couple of phone calls?"

Ask the Pencil's Deadlines and Know Yours as Well.

All meeting wrap-ups should acknowledge the Pencil's line review dates as well as your deadlines for orders/projections and should honestly address any conflicts, e.g. "Since your line review is two weeks from now and we will need quantities by this Friday in order to hit a June 1st start date, we'll either need to get some kind of advance commitment this week or look at June 15th to start shipping. What do you think?"

Observe the "One Block" Rule.

The one block rule means not saying a *word* about how the meeting went, any impressions or commentary, until you are literally one block away from the building. Remember that walls have ears and that you cannot assume whose ears are in the next room, in the hallway, in the elevator, or in the lobby on the way out. Save the high-fives (or the groans) for outside.

Pencil Pearl

As a Vice-President for a technology company, Lisa had just left a meeting with a big Pencil with her sales team. They had packed up and gone down the elevator to the lobby. As soon as the elevator doors to the lobby flew open, one of her sales reps, assuming it was safe, popped off that the Pencil was stupid for not asking for a price reduction. Well, that Pencil happened to have beaten them to the lobby and was on her way out of the building to smoke a cigarette. As Lisa disciplined the sales rep, up walked the Pencil, cigarette in hand, to say that she didn't see why she should do business with a company that wouldn't proactively offer her the best price. Ouch!

What to Avoid

Gossip

Gossiping to or with your Pencil, even when prompted, is unacceptable and will only serve to make you look unprofessional and leave your Pencil wondering what you say about them behind their back. Gossip includes negative revelations about your competition, comments about other Pencils (regardless of where they are), and negative comments about personnel within *your* organization.

Bad Language

Even if your Pencil curses like a sailor, matching the language will only make you sound coarse and once again, unprofessional. Also know that religious beliefs expand the definition of bad language. Terms like "Jesus Christ!" or "Oh, God!" can cause offense and certainly enough alternatives exist to keep from using them. We are surprised by the number of people who use "GD" constantly and believe its use is perfectly acceptable!

Bad Gender References

Female Pencils do not want to be called "girls" or "gals" (or hear other women over the age of 19 referred to that way).

Increasingly, female Pencils aren't crazy about being called "guys" either (as in "what do you guys think?").

Controversial Topics

No matter how "obvious" a point of view may seem, you can never assume that your Pencil shares it! The usual controversial topics of politics, religion, race, and sexuality should be avoided completely. Once again, never *assume* your audience.

Letting the Meeting Run Long

The old sales saw of "Use every minute they give you" too often translates to "Let it run over." We suggest proactively asking the Pencil, "We're right at the hour and I can wrap this up if you'll give me another ten minutes. Do you need to be somewhere?" Nine times out of ten, your Pencil will say, "Yes, but I can steal ten minutes if that's all you need." We go so far as to play time-keeper and propose solutions: "I know you need to get going to your meeting ..." then "... I'm going to meet with John in department 34 for an hour, if you have any time after one o'clock I'll swing back by" or "... Run off to your meeting. I'll group and mark your samples for you and drop them by your office by the end of the day. You'll have your set-up sheets within two days."

Cutting the Meeting Short

On the other hand, if your Pencil seems to want more time with you, by all means don't cut things short because you want to get home sooner or catch that early flight. Within reason, your schedule should be open. If you have another meeting in the Pencil's corporate office, offer to come back later to finish up.

Being Late

It is another rule of inequality that your Pencil can be late but you can't. If your Pencil is late to a meeting, just do your best to carry on and follow the agenda. Throughout her career, Carol has worked with Pencils who were reliably late to every single product presentation she conducted. One Pencil was exactly one and a half hours late to every meeting – you could set your watch by it. The Pencil's assistant would come down to the lobby to retrieve Carol one hour after the appointment time. Carol would be shown to the designated showroom and the Pencil would appear thirty minutes later without apology. Carol just brought lots of reading material and work projects and this became her catch-up time each week. This Pencil became Carol's highest volume department in short order.

Reluctance to Bring in Help

Bringing in help can be a show of strength. For example, "You had a lot of questions about garment construction. I'd like you to meet my designer, Mark. He could do a better job of explaining the construction of our garments and I want you to have full confidence in where we're going. What does next Wednesday look like for you?" It's a great way to show that you are listening and to have a reason for a follow-up meeting.

Selling Out Your Pencil

Never reveal your Pencil's promotional strategies, pricing, or personnel problems to other Pencils.

Chapter 12: Projections, Forecasts, Estimates, and Other Non-orders

Pencils often get blamed for canceling orders when in reality a break-down in communication occurred. In their minds, they gave a *projection* (forecast, estimate, etc.), not an order. This difficulty can crop up more frequently with organizations that utilize independent reps than with those that have direct sales representation. This is because independent reps can understandably be more focused on protecting the Pencil's needs than on managing the supplier company's inventory. While most sales representatives operate with integrity, there are those who receive quantity *projections* from their Pencils, yet communicate them to the supplier company as *orders* in hopes that eventually the quantities will be ordered and all will be fine in the end. That obviously is not the Pencil's problem!

Pencil Pearl

One of our supplier clients wanted to drill down on the reasons for mounting inventory with one of their top retailers. Carol began traveling extensively with the independent rep responsible for the account and taking detailed notes from every Pencil meeting. She began to see that her version of events was quite different from that of the rep. Not only was he placing orders for quantities that were only expressed as *estimates* by the Pencil, but he also padded the quantities in order to ensure availability. When Carol confronted him about the discrepancies, he blurted out, "I *have* to do this because they (the supplier) never put in enough inventory and it makes me look bad with my buyer — I've learned to just sell and repent!" The supplier company did have a long history of second-guessing estimates, so in a sense both parties were right. In the end they agreed to start over, with the rep honestly relaying the Pencil's exact intentions and quantities to the supplier and the supplier's purchasing department agreeing to discuss any intentions to vary.

Start-up companies can also make the mistake of assuming that a Pencil is placing an order when in reality, he or she giving an estimate or a projection. When meeting with a Pencil, or in your follow up (whenever the conversation regarding quantities takes place), it is important to clarify your Pencil's intentions. Any time your Pencil gives a quantity, you should ask, "Is that a firm order or a projection?" She may respond simply, "It's an order; I'll put a P.O. in for it next week." She may also say, "Well, I don't see any reason why the stores wouldn't order at least that much." That means it is a projection.

Start-up suppliers also can become overly concerned with the difference between orders and projections, thinking that responsibility changes accordingly. The fact is, even if a Pencil give you a firm order, if the product doesn't sell they will still generally consider it your responsibility to take care of it either by giving them mark-down money (money at the end of the selling season that will make up the difference between their needed sales and what actually happened), or by offering other discounts or even merchandise returns.

It used to be that a Pencil took full responsibility for the quantities ordered. She chose the trends to follow and bought as if she believed in it. If the product didn't sell, she was charged with reducing the price to clear it out and had to live with the resulting reduced profit margins in her department. These days, Pencils make the rounds at the end of a selling season (sometimes even before it is over, based on how sales are trending), to get mark-down money from their suppliers. This process has become so automatic with some retailers that suppliers *expect* to be approached, even for items that sold relatively well. Some Pencils now look at their overall profitability and expect their suppliers to offset a percentage of it (regardless of how their items performed).

This sounds pretty ominous and it is, for suppliers who don't keep good records, don't price their products thoughtfully, and don't follow sales performance!

Pencil Point # 38

These days, inventory shortages or overages tend to become the supplier's responsibility regardless of whether they originated as a firm order or as a projection, forecast, or estimate.

The difference between projections and firm orders matters most from a supplier-forecasting standpoint. If you have the *assumptions* behind any initial orders or projections, then you are armed with information that will keep the Pencil in stock with your item(s). This is why we recommend that start-up suppliers hire a forecaster-analyst even before they bring in sales help. A qualified analyst will not only be able to translate sales data generated by your Pencil, but will be able to use that information to help you project your inventory needs.

A typical scenario might go something like this:

Your Pencil gives you a firm order to set the stores (sometimes called a "set order"). That order will be transmitted electronically to your company to trigger shipping to various distribution centers. Once the orders are set with your product, replenishment orders will be generated automatically at intervals (weekly, monthly, or at random, depending on the retailer) based on sales. You will be responsible for keeping the stores in stock for the duration of the program.

This is one of many possible scenarios (including one-time orders that have no replenishment). We won't go into all of them since what is important is to get the information you need in order to know what the Pencil's expectations are. We have worked with start-up suppliers who built up tons of inventory in anticipation of orders that the Pencil never intended to place and have worked with others who built no additional inventory and were blamed for omissions.

When the conversation turns to quantities, make sure you can answer the following questions:

- How long is the program (how long does the Pencil want this product to remain in the selected stores)?
- How many weeks of supply does your Pencil like to keep on hand?
- How many stores are planned for this product (don't assume it's an "all-store" buy)?
- What is the minimum quantity for replenishment (how many units are in a minimum pack for the store)?
- What are their standards for sales (do they look at sales per store per week or a percentage sell-through per week), and what constitutes good sales for an item (is it one per store per week, 5% sell-through per week, etc.)?

Don't let the process and terminology intimidate you. With qualified help on board or outsourced, you will navigate these questions and protect yourself in the process. Once you have this information, you are better equipped to partner with your Pencil to keep your product in the stores by clearly understanding their intentions and by reacting to sales.

Pencil Point # 39

Understanding your Pencil's intentions for your product is of utmost importance. You can then partner with them to maximize opportunities.

Chapter 13: Pencil Follow-Up

You've finished the meeting and are heading back to the home office. You are still very much at the true beginning of the sales process and what you do from this point on will in large part determine your success or failure with your Pencils. The time span between *show* and *commit* may be only a week, or it may be more than a month; however, the way you handle inquiries and requirements in the meantime will say a lot about your overall capabilities.

It can be frustrating to leave a meeting high-fiving your colleagues one minute then, a month later, hear your Pencil ask, "Did I see that sample?" You've been patiently (or not so patiently), waiting to hear back and they don't even remember what they saw? Thus begins the process of professional follow-up, the fundamental premise of which is to use every opportunity to make your Pencil's job easier (and therefore make it easier to buy your products)!

The first step in effective meeting follow-up has already been addressed: leaving behind the best possible memory of your presentation in the form of an integrated package of samples, photos, plan-o-grams, and pricing. Step two is to fully document the meeting within your company and back to your Pencil.

Thorough and frequent communication back to your Pencils is one of the most valuable tools to minimize charge-backs, inventory-related problems, and general misunderstandings; and yet, as mentioned before, many salespeople and sales managers continue to rely on verbal, or poorly-composed e-mail and written, confirmations. In our many years of sales management and consulting work, we have seen how one incident of poor external documentation can create problems so complex that they seem, at the end, to have many origins. In fact, many can be traced to a single undocumented assumption or poorly documented intention.

Documenting to Your Pencil

After you meet with a Pencil, even as a start-up company, you should re-cap your understanding of the meeting back to the Pencil. Depending on time frame, we would suggest an e-mail with a professional letter follow-up. That documentation should include a re-cap of:

- Items of interest referencing item numbers, descriptions, and costs (and quantities, if any were provided)
- Agreed time frames
- Any requested changes
- Agreed follow-up

A sample e-mail might read:

Subject: MEETING FOLLOW-UP

Dear Ms. Abernathy:

It was a pleasure meeting with you yesterday and getting your thoughts on our children's hats.

I have attached a spreadsheet confirming your items of interest, including style numbers, descriptions, cost, and which samples were left with you.

As we discussed, we are going to add green and blue to style number 87364 and will have samples to you by Friday of next week, along with samples of styles 87382 and 87390 in fleece (you have samples of knit).

I look forward to hearing the results of your line review and, as we discussed, I will follow up on June 7th to discuss status if I don't hear from you before. In the meantime, please do not hesitate to contact me with any questions or needs.

Thank you for your consideration.

The typed letter, on company letterhead, can contain a bit more content, such as "I appreciated your comments regarding. . ." or, "I believe we have a great opportunity ..."

Pencil Point # 40

Pencils prefer that e-mails cut to the chase.

Professional Pencil Communication

Business communication and correspondence, especially within vendor companies, has become distressingly unprofessional, casual, and downright inept in many cases. We attribute this to a few causes:

- Professionally trained secretaries are increasingly rare. There is no longer a central approval point for company correspondence. This results in errors and inconsistent and/or poor formatting.

- E-mail has become an easy way to communicate, and company principals have allowed bad grammar, spelling errors, and slang (including their own), to be unleashed on their customers in the interest of "efficiency."

- Vendors often believe that they are friendly with their Pencils and forget that the Pencil is *the customer*.

- Sales training is virtually unheard of in the vendor community. Therefore, sales people (and company principals), tend to communicate the way they always have (which may never have involved professional correspondence skills).

- Just as with dress, vendors mistakenly believe that mirroring the communication style of their Pencil (however casual or abrupt), is more appropriate than maintaining consistent standards.

- Centralized networked printers can make writing professional letters on company letterhead a chore.

Pencil Pearl

We had an ongoing relationship with one company principal who, when we first met him, was sitting in his trade show booth, *smoking* (in a non-smoking building), with his tie askew, his shoes scuffed, and a big stain on his shirt. Appearances aside, he was a terribly astute businessman who cared deeply about his customers and his business (and his sales volume certainly reflected this). We noticed that all correspondence from his company was professional, clear, and concise and that his follow-up was always courteous and prompt. One day, he commented on what a completely disorganized mess he was. We gave him credit for all of the positives mentioned previously and he replied with a laugh, "Don't give *me* credit for that! I have Kathy to thank. I call her (his executive assistant) the 'Vice President of Everything' because I can barely write a sentence ... Nothing goes out from me unless it goes through her ... I'm smart enough to know what I'm good at and where I need help."

Smart indeed!

Written Correspondence

- *Anything larger than a Post-it-Note® should be typed* – The only exception would be personal thank-you notes. Scribbling notes to Pencils looks terribly unprofessional, especially when anyone and everyone has access to a computer and a printer!

- *Standard business formats should be utilized* – That's right, a date, address block, and "Dear (so and so)," ending with "Sincerely" and your typed name with a signature above. This is not a hassle if you create pre-set templates for each account with margins pre-set for your company's letterhead. For short notes, utilize notepaper with your company logo and name on it.

- *Fill out all Pencil-generated forms completely and accurately* – Set-up sheets, product testing sheets, specification sheets ... all should be filled out as completely, accurately, and neatly as possible. Ask your Pencil early on whom their preferred contact person is for any inquiries (don't keep calling your Pencil to ask "what do I put in line 32?" if he/she has referred you to someone else within their organization). Either print out or make copies of everything sent out.

E-Mail Communication

- *Create an informative at-a-glance subject line* – The subject "SAMPLE AVAILABILITY FROM OUR 7-2 MEETING" is much more helpful than "PLEASE GET BACK TO ME" or "I NEED AN ANSWER."

- *Use Appropriate Salutations* – We are shocked at how many vendors use greetings like "Hey," "Hi There," "Hi," "What's Up?" etc. This is a *customer*, not your buddy. Show respect by beginning initial contact with "Dear Marcie" and for ongoing replies to the same e-mail, "Marcie."

- *Keep initial communication formal* – Never call a Pencil by their first name in an introduction letter. It is "Dear Ms. Jones" until you establish familiar terms. This will get you noticed quicker than anything since no one does it anymore!

- *Keep it to the point but include enough information* – Give the Pencil enough information to respond with a definitive answer. The difference between "Jane, the vessel containing your hats sank in the harbor and we really need to talk soon about what to do." and "Jane, we need an extension on P.O. # 02984317 from a start ship of 01/05 to 01/15 start ship date. If you approve the extension today, we'll hit your anniversary sale" is about five e-mails!

- *Use "cc" and forwarding logically* – How many times have we received e-mails not meant for our eyes sent to us as a "forward?" Look at the ENTIRE contents of an e-mail and all exchanges included before determining if it is appropriate to send. Don't "cc" the universe on everything you send. Utilize "bcc" (blind copy) in order to protect distribution.

- *Watch for e-mail address defaults* – e-mail has become intuitive to a fault so double-check all recipients to make sure the computer guessed correctly!

- *Don't forward inspirational, "funny" or political e-mails* – In short, if it isn't business-related, don't send it. Even if your Pencil forwards such e-mails to you, don't reciprocate.

It's just plain unprofessional and makes you look like you have too much time on your hands.

- *Don't abbreviate anything unless it is truly an acronym* – Do not type "tx" for "thank you," "BTW" for "by the way," "u" for "you," etc. Again, you are corresponding with a *customer*. Using abbreviations is lazy, unprofessional, and far too casual for your valued Pencils.

- *Insert a signature block* – Create a signature block that automatically appears whenever you compose or respond to an e-mail. This should include, at the minimum, your name, company name, and phone number, but can also include your title and web site address.

- *Use appropriate formats* – If documentation requires that columns of information be related ("style #," "description," "cost"), don't attempt to "tab over" within the body of an e-mail. You will run the risk of losing your formatting (and the person on the other end seeing a block of undecipherable characters). Take the time to create and attach a spreadsheet!

Written and E-mail Communication

- *Avoid icons, exaggerated punctuation and other attention-grabbers* – "YELLING" all capital letters is completely unacceptable, as is using infantile, all lower case. Use the "shift" key and forget the "smiley."

- *Avoid odd or clever fonts*

- *Don't mirror your Pencil's style (or lack of)* – Just because your Pencil hand-writes notes to you that begin "Hey,

Jane" doesn't mean your response shouldn't be a typed "Dear Marcie ... "

- *Use spell-check, and then check again* – Misspellings and grammar mistakes in e-mails and written communication send such a negative message to your Pencils. To be blunt, they make you look unintelligent and make your Pencils wonder if you are on the ball with other aspects of the business. As great a feature as spell-check is, it doesn't catch everything (and misreads others). Use the spell-check features on your computer and read everything twice before sending.

- *Pick your spots and don't "bunt" the Pencil* - One of the top peeves that Pencils share with us is over-communicating. Think twice before firing off e-mails. Can it wait until the end of the day and be added to another e-mail? Is it something you can handle without the Pencil? Is it more appropriate for the Pencil's assistant? Remember, as important as your Pencil is to you, they are dealing with LOTS of "*you*'s!"

Phone Communication

- *Answer the phone professionally, pleasantly, and consistently* – Your phone greeting shouldn't change according to your mood, your workload, etc. Examples of good greetings are "Fantastic Hats, this is Janie," or "Hello, this is Janie." Examples of unprofessional greetings are "Yes," "Yeah," "Hey," "Hey, this is Janie," "Hi ..." and we could go on. We knew a salesman (who was actually one of the nicest guys we've met in the business), who had a habit of saying "What's up?" as his second line (after "Hey"). It had the unintended effect of sounding like "Can we get on with this? I'm busy."

- *When you call a Pencil, ask if they have time* – One of the more astute salespeople that Carol had the privilege of managing used to begin every conversation with "Did I catch you at a good time?" Nothing is worse than launching into a diatribe about why you called only to have your Pencil say, "I'm in a meeting!"

- *Never use caller ID* – If your office has caller ID, never answer the phone based on who you assume is on the other line. Answering, "Hi, John" or "I knew you'd call" is completely unprofessional. Invariably, if you get in the habit of using caller ID to customize your response, you'll end up saying "Hey, Babe" to your top Pencil (Who knew the name of the Pencil's company had so many letters in common with your wife's company?).

- *Always close the conversation* – Never just hang up the phone. Say "thanks, good bye."

Pencil Point # 41

*Create **standards** for communication and stick to them. Consistency counts!*

Observe Pencil Patterns

After a few weeks or even days of working with a Pencil, you will begin to spot patterns of style and preference. Too many suppliers ignore these patterns, much to the frustration of their Pencils. If a Pencil, after a meeting, always asks you to send samples of all styles of interest, then end the meeting with "Marcie, I'll get samples to you by the end of next week," not "So, do you want me to sample *everything*?" If your Pencil always reviews business before looking at samples, start the meeting off that way. If your Pencil asks you to fill out all forms in blue ink, by all means, buy boxes of blue pens! We have been in meetings in which Pencils have asked salespeople, "Why do I have to ask you this, John? I've been doing it this way for five years."

"I went ahead and sent that Fed-Ex ... we shipped those samples three days early to make sure you had them before your line review," and "Oh, I don't need any set-up sheets. I have copies of them at my office and will get them back to you tomorrow." All music to a Pencil's ears!

Pencil Point # 42

Taking an intuitive and proactive approach with your Pencil will put you ahead of the pack.

Importance of Quick Response

Any time your Pencil assigns a deadline, regardless of whether you agree with it or not, you must acknowledge the deadline. This sounds simple enough, yet suppliers still play the waiting game, especially with difficult requests. It used to be that when a Pencil asked for something like mark-down money, suppliers would try to wait it out in hopes that the Pencil would forget the request, or at least realize that the supplier was in no hurry, or wasn't an easy target. These days, other suppliers are competing with you — suppliers who respond quickly to such requests. You gain nothing by delaying your response (except the Pencil's ire). If you disagree with a request or need to negotiate, do so before the deadline. Just as with other special requests, it's not personal. The Pencil is doing her job and unresponsive suppliers create a double-whammy for the Pencil. Not only are you alienating her, but you are making her look bad to management. She will have a hard time forgetting that you put her in such a position!

Now is as good a time as any to bring up the topic of availability. These days, there is no excuse for not checking e-mail and voice mail while you are traveling (except on vacation). You may still get away with it, but it will make you look unprofessional. On the other hand, Pencils are impressed when you get back to them while you are on the road. Don't hesitate to tell them that you're sorry you didn't get back to them that morning, you just arrived in Chicago.

Pencil Point # 43

Lack of response or slow response achieves nothing except to make your organization look unprofessional.

Chapter 14: Internal Follow-Up

As mentioned previously, Pencils continue to delegate more administrative tasks to their suppliers. Lean and mean start-up companies can't afford to ignore this fact by hiring personnel who aren't up to the task, and sales managers and salespeople should never believe that documentation is beneath them. Anyone on the front line is responsible for informing all relevant supplier departments in writing of what happened during a key Pencil meeting and fully addressing all pencil-assigned tasks.

This becomes especially pressing when you consider shorter lead times and the need for everyone to get going on *their* part of making things happen.

Pencil meetings immediately lengthen a salesperson's "to do" list, and it can be tempting to just tell people back at the supplier office what happened at a meeting. We have seen major mistakes happen when suppliers operate from verbal re-caps. The Product person runs back to the office and starts work on product concepts based on their understanding of the facts. Business Planning begins ordering based on *their* understanding. When the written re-cap is finally distributed, everyone ignores it as "unnecessary." The salesperson assumes that the written re-cap cleared up any mistakes made in their verbal re-cap, and everyone moves on doing the wrong thing without any evidence of original intentions.

Refer to your notes, get the facts straight, compile a report, and distribute it as soon as possible in order to avoid misinterpretation or delay. If you have any questions whatsoever regarding agreed action steps, ask your Pencil for clarification (never guess). We always liked to create re-caps on the plane, and then e-mail them immediately when we got to the nearest dial-up connection. Following this example, you can greet everyone at the office with "did you get my re-cap?" and can go on about your business.

For start-up companies that don't yet have a developed organization, we still recommend getting into the documentation habit early.

Pencil Point # 44

Your memory of meetings will fade fast and you'll need to refer back to your notes more often than you think, especially as your business grows!

Pencil Pearl

After conducting an organizational assessment and retailer surveys for one of our client companies, we realized that most of their profit-erosion problems and Pencil conflicts could be traced to poor documentation and communication. The company principal believed that communication *couldn't* be consistent since they used a combination of independent and direct sales representatives. We worked with him to establish corporate templates and standards for communication, and conducted our "Cleaning up Communication" seminar for the company's internal personnel. At our six-month check-up, punitive charges had been reduced by 30%, and the supplier's top Pencils expressed relief over the improved quality and reduced *quantity* of communication.

We encourage our client companies to develop templates that will standardize the communication process and make it easier for everyone to look for information that pertains to them. If the salesperson responsible for the account reports to the vendor office, that salesperson should take the additional step of calling a team meeting to review the written re-cap in person with all departments involved. These meetings bring the added benefit of fostering cooperation and communication between departments. With today's high-volume, high-door-count businesses, these steps are not overkill, they provide *necessary* checks and balances and clarity on the front end (when changes can still be made). Countless costly charge-backs, shipping delays, and inventory problems can be avoided simply by beginning the internal checks and balances as early as possible.

SAMPLE MEETING RE-CAP
(Suggested template headings in bold)

ACCOUNT: WAL-MART

DATE: 1-11-05

PURPOSE: Fall 06 Hat Presentation

IN ATTENDANCE:

Wal-Mart: John Jackson, Buyer, Jane Simpson, Business Planner

Fantastic Hats: Mary Lou, Sales, Bob, Planner

GENERAL

The meeting was very positive and we covered a lot of ground. The great news is that we have been chosen once again to supply product for the new "Hats Off" end cap for fall (see specific notes below). John gave initial commitments for fall styles (see attached), and indicated that we may be considered for their Holiday promotion (see meeting scheduled for concept presentation below).

PURCHASING REVIEW

Jane asked that we take a look at style 45903 and get back to her as soon as possible on when we can get additional quantities. She said she would order whatever we have. Let's discuss what we can do and I will relay that back to her.

John gave initial projections for fall 6-1 core styles (attached), and will provide remaining deliveries no later than 2-1-05.

PURCHASING TOPICS

Sales for style 89765 have slowed down and Jane asked that we not order any more. At this point, they are willing to try and sell down on it. I show that we have 10,000 units on hand right now. Let's discuss what we can do with those quantities since they won't be sending any more orders.

KEY DATES

1-13-05 (tomorrow), information on additional quantities available for style 45903 and dates.

2-1-05 Deadline for additional quantities from John for remaining fall deliveries.

This week's re-cap meeting (day TBD): Discuss 89765 inventory and sell-down.

PRODUCT REVIEW

John commented that our colors for the season were right on. He wants to use most of them as fall core colors then have us work with their program colors for the "hats off" end cap (see dates below). John said we could have our "one of a kind" samples back next Friday (pick them up when we are in their offices for the seminar).

PRODUCT TOPICS

Returns on style 87693 have increased this week (three times that of any other style in the group). We need to pull production and see what the problem might be.

KEY DATES

1-15-05: Get back to John on possible quality/color problem on style 87693.

1-20-05: Remaining samples due for fall '05 (see sample request attached for samples not left at meeting).

Week of 1-24-05: Pantones and swatches available for "Hats Off" program colors.

2-15-03 Meeting with John to present Holiday concepts.

Ongoing Internal and External Communication

In today's world of punitive charge-backs and retailer-specific policies, *ongoing* documentation is a must, to include:

External

- Any changes to style numbers, cost, colors, descriptions
- Any changes to style availability
- Requests for order extensions
- Approval of order extensions
- Increases or decreases in style quantities on-order (however initiated)
- Increases or decreases to company forecasts that affect your Pencil

External and Internal

- Requests for order extensions
- Approval of order extensions
- Increases or decreases in style quantities on-order (however initiated)
- Increases or decreases to company forecast that affects your Pencil

Pencil Point # 45

Documentation plays a huge role in today's retail environment. Leave nothing to chance and get everyone into the documentation habit.

Chapter 15: Understanding Pencil Hierarchy

Many start-ups ask us to outline who does what within retail organizations. The answers vary greatly by retailer and by department within each retailer, and it will continue to change based on category volume and Pencil preferences.

In smaller-volume retailers, a Pencil may buy all categories for the store and not have assistants; in medium-sized operations, several buyers may cover all categories, and those with the highest-volume departments will have assistants while the others may not.

It is important to know that, regardless of title, some categories are bought by assistant buyers, not the senior buyer for a department. Categories such as accessories that are bought in relation to core items are a good example. The buyer buys the core category and delegates accessories to the assistant buyer. Suppliers make a big mistake when they constantly try to go over the assistant buyer's head in such situations. If a buyer has made it clear that they want you to work with the assistant, then treat that assistant as the buyer, never go over their head, and enjoy whatever time the buyer gives to you. There is no shame in working with assistants. Know that the buyer is monitoring things and will respect you for honoring their wishes. Most buyers, even those who may seem harsh, cannot stand it when suppliers mistreat or disregard people on their team.

Pencil Point # 46

Never demand buyer involvement. Work professionally and courteously with whoever is assigned to you.

Assistants - Your Greatest Ally

"Did you get the samples I sent?" "What am I supposed to put in line 32 of your item set-up sheet?" "Is your line review over?" All great questions for your Pencil's assistant! Generally, the more details you take away from your main Pencil, the more you will be appreciated and respected. We know established suppliers who just can't seem to get it into their heads that the buyer does not want to handle any and every inquiry. As a result, when they really do need the top Pencil's attention, it is rarely given!

Anytime you call the Pencil office and the assistant picks up, acknowledge them and ask respectfully if you may speak to the main Pencil. Never blurt out, "I need to speak to Marcie." Trust us, one day that assistant will become a buyer and they always remember those who gave them respect early on. On the other hand, you never want to waste an assistant's or a buyer's time with excessive chit chat – Pencils tell us that suppliers who have that reputation are avoided at all costs, and communication switches to e-mail.

If an assistant is present during your product presentation, copy that person on your correspondence as well. From that point on, they may become your primary contact.

In general, you should make it your goal to become acquainted with as many assistants and support staff as possible at the Pencil office. When you DO need your Pencil's attention, those relationships will come in handy. Every now and then you may find yourself asking the assistant, "I wouldn't normally do this but Marcie hasn't returned my call and we are going to miss her July shipments if we don't get an answer. Is there any way I can ask you to tap her on the shoulder? Thanks so much."

Pencil Point # 47

Assistants become buyers. Treat them with respect!

Chapter 16: They Love Me ... They Love Me <u>Not</u>?

You had a great meeting, you followed up with samples on time, and you filled out the forms and made all requested changes. It's two months later and you check in with the Pencil to ask how the line review went. They send an e-mail that says, "I liked your hats a lot but after showing them to my management and discussing our direction for fall, we don't see using your products at this time. I'll keep your information on file and let you know if any opportunities come up."

Keep your cool and remember that selling to Pencils is often a *process*. You may feel that you put forth a lot of effort to get such a return, but now more than ever it's time to exhibit restraint and professionalism. The cooler you are about this disappointment, the better your chances of getting your product placed with that Pencil in the future.

An appropriate response to that e-mail might be:

Dear Marcie:

Obviously this is a disappointment but I appreciate your consideration and your input regarding our products. It was a pleasure meeting you and I trust that you will keep us in mind for future opportunities.

You indicated that your planning for Holiday would begin in April. I'd like to follow up with you then to show our line updates.

In the meantime, please don't hesitate to contact me if you see opportunities for our hats.

Thank you again for your consideration.

We would also recommend sending a note to the Pencil's assistant (if you had any contact with them). You might write:

Dear Laura:

By now, I'm sure you know that we were not chosen in your fall line review. I just wanted to thank you for your help and for walking us through your procedures. Your patience and professionalism were very much appreciated by my staff and me. As I mentioned to Marcie, we would welcome the opportunity to work with you in the future and appreciate your keeping our products in mind for any opportunities.

Best Regards,

Pencil Pearl

Back in her sales days, Carol had shown the products, executed all of the required follow-up, and was awaiting results from a top mass retail Pencil. After what seemed like ages, the buyer sent a curt response that none of Carol's products were chosen. Carol sent a professional response and called the Pencil a couple of months later when the new season was being planned. The Pencil asked, "What makes you think I'll be any more interested than I was last time?" Carol kept her cool and replied, "I have no idea, but I'd like to try again." The Pencil gave her an appointment, and Carol went through all of the follow-up, thinking probably nothing would come of it, that is until a phone message appeared during a subsequent business trip. Carol returned the phone call from an airplane. On the other end, the Pencil said, "I've got five minutes to give you these quantities so start writing." Carol took the order and after hanging up, did a quick calculation ... three million dollars. She went on to grow business with this Pencil to over eleven million dollars. After Carol had passed the Pencil's test of fire, the Pencil told her she gave Carol early points for keeping her cool, remaining professional, and following up again ... "You'd be surprised how many people don't do that," Carol's buyer later remarked.

Never assume that a door will *remain* closed. Whenever you get a meeting with a Pencil, always make sure to get the timing for their *next* planning season. This information will come in handy, regardless of the outcome of your current initiative.

Chapter 17: Other Types of Meetings

Product meetings aren't the only ones you will be attending in the course of doing business with major retailers and licensors. Today's world of retailing offers innumerable opportunities for vendor summits, conventions, and other retailer and licensor-sponsored events.

Notice we use the word "opportunities." Many established vendor companies develop an attitude about these events that is completely counter-productive. They balk at the cost of participation (travel expenses, time out of the office, and fees for attendance), then send support personnel to cover the event, rather than taking full advantage of the opportunity for more face-time with their top Pencils!

In our experience, established companies will be hard-pressed to find better venues for networking with upper-level retail and licensing management and should not underestimate the value of full participation. Conversely, start-up companies can make the mistake of over-investing in trade-show participation, believing that it is the best way to get discovered. Often they embark on establishing a trade-show presence before they are fully prepared or before they understand the costs and benefits of a given show. In general, start-up companies should accept any invitations to retailer or licensor-sponsored events but should weigh the costs and benefits of trade show attendance.

Trade shows

A tradeshow is a vendor event in which your company sets up a booth or showroom and welcomes the trade to drop by.

As a start-up, you answer the following questions before deciding on pursuing a trade show presence:

- Who is the show targeted to and will participation further my distribution goals? As mentioned earlier in the book, many major retailers no longer attend trade shows and most shows primarily target specialty stores. If your goal is to distribute your products through specialty stores, trade shows are a good strategy. Do not invest in a trade show booth hoping that a major retailer will stop by and notice your product (unless you have a set appointment with them). It can happen but often does not!

- Is my product ready and can I answer all of the questions in newmarketbuilders' "Are You Really Ready for Retailers?" checklist (Chapter Three)?

- Would I be better off attending the show (for ideas and networking) rather than exhibiting?

Whether you are an established vendor who regularly attends trade shows or a start-up seeking increased visibility, consider the following when setting up and working the show:

- *Set up the show with a "Reason to Be" and set up appointments under the same premise* – Are you showing something truly unique that warrants a visit? Pencils are busy at shows and will want to have a compelling reason to visit. If you were at their offices just a week ago, asking them for a trade show appointment may result in a no-show. Don't bully your Pencils into coming by your showroom if there isn't a compelling reason for them to do so.

- *Consider a non-sales premise for trade show appointments* – Trade shows present an excellent opportunity to get early buy-in on next season's concepts and to conduct business reviews with your current customers (with samples at the ready).

- *Bring your best* – If you are going to make the investment in the space then you should also invest in the appearance and quality of the booth, marketing materials and those occupying the space. Sloppy, cheap, or half-baked handouts and business cards are not worth the effort or expense and they send a bad message about your company. The same goes for unprofessional personnel.

- *Avoid the used-car-lot syndrome* – Nothing is less inviting to a Pencil than a group of salespeople blocking a booth entrance and talking among themselves, or salespeople staring down any and all walk-ins. Break up the crowd and see that every Pencil is greeted pleasantly and professionally, and then escorted to wherever they need to be.

- *Consider utilizing a multilingual resource* – Having a Spanish-speaking, or other language resource on hand is increasingly appropriate and appreciated, depending on the demographics and geography covered by the show.

- *Keep the principals around* – Yes, trade shows can be terrifically boring and it is tempting to spend much of the time on a cell phone, shopping at local venues, or at the café. Countless opportunities are missed that way.

- *Greet everyone as though they matter* - Treat everyone who walks into your booth or showroom as somebody special and don't assume you know to whom you're speaking.

- *Carefully consider "drop-by" advertising pitches (for start-ups)* – We've noticed an increase in magazine advertising pitches at trade shows. Often, start-ups are flattered that a major consumer publication dropped by, complimented their products, and offered special rates on advertising. While consumer advertising may play a role as a secondary strategy for more developed companies, start-ups should remember that their primary customer is the Pencil (not the consumer).

Vendor Summits and Vendor Training Sessions

Vendor summits and vendor training sessions are invitation-only meetings with your retailer where you sit thigh-to-thigh with your competition and interact regarding store initiatives and processes.

These meetings can be nail-biters that have everyone wondering and worrying about what information to share or hold back and various vendors vying for Pencil attention and recognition.

The following are suggestions that will help you get the most out of all non-product meetings (and help you get invited again next time).

- *Meet and greet* – Don't stay in your corporate clique and look the rest of the crowd up and down. Introduce yourself and greet others, especially those who appear to be there for the first time, or attending alone.

- *Be positive* – Don't complain to other attendees about being there, about meeting content, or about others in attendance (Pencils or vendors).

- *Don't buttonhole your Pencils* – Your Pencils will be busy coordinating the event, circulating, and keeping everything in order, and won't appreciate being cornered. Greet them pleasantly and let them off the hook (they will appreciate it). Even if your Pencil seems to be engaged with a competing vendor, resist the temptation to compete for attention and, instead, stay with the purpose of the meeting and focus on making it productive for your company and for others in attendance.

- *Frame your questions and points* – Use diplomacy when asking questions or making points. Avoid accusatory, whiney, or inflammatory tones.

- *Don't dominate the meeting* – Avoid dominating the meeting either by over-participating (not letting others have a chance), by being long-winded, or by demanding attention to your specific topics (ones that have no relevance to the rest of the group). You don't have to be continually heard in order to be seen.

- *Pay attention* – Show respect for your meeting hosts by turning off your cell phone and PDA, staying put, and paying attention (not working on other projects or looking at other materials).

- *Stick it out* – Plan your flights and other meetings in advance and don't be the one (or one of the few), who has to disrupt the meeting by dashing out early.

- *Look your best* – If the meeting is business casual, that doesn't necessarily mean *your* company's version of business casual. Dress up a notch. It certainly can't hurt!

- *Bring your best* – Look at the pre-meeting materials and bring the appropriate personnel. If your Pencil has indicated that analytical and warehouse personnel are appropriate, don't send the showroom assistant to take notes and bring information back to the office. When possible, add a company principal or top manager to the meeting. You will be seen as a hands-on owner or manager who isn't above getting involved, and regular participation in such events helps keep you out of the ivory tower.

Conventions

By conventions, we are referring to small or large-scale invitation-only events where vendors set up products for viewing by Pencil store managers or personnel. To the previous suggestions, we would add:

- *Show up* – Nothing will get your company more noticed in a negative way than not showing up and expecting your Pencils or (heaven forbid) competing vendors to set up your product for you. Rearrange your schedule and get to the convention.

- *Send materials and follow up* – Send the requested number of samples ahead of time or bring them with you. If sent ahead of time, track and follow up on the shipments (don't just assume they arrived at their destination).

- *Follow the rules* – Honor all set-up times and procedures. If set-up is stated as "Wednesday morning," don't arrive Wednesday night and hope to set up on Thursday morning.

- *Stick it out* – We'll reiterate this point specific to conventions. Many vendor companies make the mistake of sending support personnel for the sample set-up portion of the meeting, and then the company principals show up at the last minute to enjoy the round-up event and speaker session. Where do you think you will be more visible — in a one-or two-day-long sample set up with constant exposure to all levels of Pencils — or sitting in a crowded auditorium and then heading to the airport?

- *Stay late and help out* – When you have finished setting up your product, don't head for the door. Ask your Pencil or competing vendor how you can help finish up. This makes an incredible impression and you'll learn a thing or two in the process. These are two to three high-exposure days out of your life. Make the most of them without complaint!

- *Don't be lazy* – Pencils and other vendors notice when half your time is spent on your cell phone or at the café. Act as though your company's reputation is at stake the entire time you are there.

Licensing Meetings

Licensing meetings are those held by major licensing entities to discuss new initiatives and review objectives. They may be held one-on-one or in group settings with other licensees. In addition to rules noted up to this point, do the following:

- *Come prepared* – Again, look through all pre-meeting information and come prepared with any and all reports and documentation requested.

- *Bring the right people* – We're stating this again. Look at the meeting materials and invite the requested personnel. When in doubt, ask your licensor Pencils who they would like to see at the meeting from your organization (you might be surprised).

- *Offer assistance with set-up* – Licensing meetings can be a bit more fluid in terms of who sets up product. It never hurts to offer one of your staff (or yourself), to help with this process prior to the meeting.

- *Take it outside* – If you have problems or complaints that are particular to your business (and think about it before you pipe up) consider discussing those outside of the group meeting. Any and all questions and comments shared in a group setting should benefit the group.

Licensing or Retailer Tele-Conferences

Tele-conferences are becoming more common as a way for groups of licensees to get together without leaving the office. Generally, most of the rules for vendor summits apply, with a few additions:

- If you are having difficulty dialing up, a slow connection etc., that is your problem. Express the difficulty once and, if you can't clear it up, offer to drop the line and reschedule. Do not attempt to take on such calls on alternative slow lines (at home), or in dicey locations.

- Keep background noise to a minimum. When you aren't talking, put on your "mute" button. We have heard everything from barking dogs, to paper stacking, to keyboard typing booming through on such calls. Very annoying to other participants.

Seminars and Other Events

Seminars and other events will be our catchall category for those increasingly rare (dying?) off-site golfing or resort meetings. All of the same rules noted above apply, with extra emphasis on dressing appropriately, showing up, and avoiding gossip. Don't underestimate the importance of table manners and etiquette and don't have *your* name on this year's embarrassing convention story!

Pencil Point # 48

All face-time with your Pencils provides an opportunity to demonstrate your professionalism, conflict resolution skills, product knowledge, and concern for your Pencil relationships. Meetings form the core of your company's overall business strategy. Don't waste a single opportunity by being reluctant, unprepared, or unprofessional.

Chapter 18: Ready!

Your Critical Success Qualities

In addition to providing strategy for start-up companies, we are often called on the scene by established vendors when one or more of the following occur:

- A key program or license gets taken away from them
- A top retailer drops them as a supplier
- Their overall business begins to go south after a period of success (sometimes a decade or more)
- Employee morale and retention begin to crumble

... and many of our clients call us in periodically and preemptively for check-ups, even when everything seems to be running smoothly. Business has never been better and they want to keep it that way! Bottom line: in years of consulting with supplier organizations and in our previous experience building multi-million-dollar sales successes for major retail vendors, certain truths have emerged regarding what it takes to succeed as a retail vendor. As mentioned previously, many suppliers are able to leverage a few key strengths (sourcing usually being one of them) toward initial retail success.

However, breakdowns begin to occur when suppliers haven't planned their business and their processes thoughtfully and, as their business grows, they apply band-aids.

If you are a current supplier, you owe it to yourself to periodically assess your company's buyer relationships, overall performance, and readiness for future opportunities (distribution, line extension, licensing). Many companies wait until symptoms appear before they take action, and their fear of change keeps them moving myopically forward. An experienced third party will be able to provide an objective evaluation and recommendations, while you and your employees go about your usual business. We can't tell you how many company principals have told us they wished they had started the process early rather than waiting until something happened!

Those of you who are start-up companies have an opportunity to do things right from the start by using the principles outlined in this book and by honestly assessing your strengths, weaknesses, and desire to move forward accordingly.

We always tell start-ups that, if their products truly fill a need, there are more options than ever for realizing incremental sales via a company website, eBay, or small trade and craft shows. There is no shame in exploring these options first, since they may help you work out the bugs and better prepare you to try again with retailers. It *is* a shame when start-up company principles don't know when to quit, and sink their life savings or those of their families into ill-conceived ventures!

Regardless of the products that you sell or aspire to sell to retailers, we believe that the following should be considered your critical success qualities. You are:

- Willing to embrace change
- Realistic about the investment and time required
- Willing to bring in help
- Willing to listen to customers and others who know
- Proactive rather than reactive
- Staying abreast of technology
- Active in maintaining a breadth of retail knowledge (by asking questions, reading trade and business publications and shopping stores)
- A user of market research prior to developing pricing, packaging and new products (not wasting resources by taking a stab or making assumptions)
- Thoughtful in considering Pencil and employee feedback and looking for patterns that may mean trouble down the line
- Aware that initial placement is only the first step

If you are willing to do all of the above, it would be hard to bet against your success ... it would be our wager that you are truly "really ready for retailers!"

Blessings,
Carol and Lisa
newmarketbuilders

Appendix 1. Pencil Points

Pencil Point # 1: Pencil organizations have become quite complex and, as a result, selling to major Pencils has never required more skill.

Pencil Point # 2: Pencils are committed to doing more business with fewer suppliers (rather than seeking new product resources).

Pencil Point # 3: The Pencil, not the consumer, is your primary customer.

Pencil Point # 4: No two retail buying structures are exactly the same.

Pencil Point # 5: If your product isn't currently in the market, you owe it to yourself to find out why before investing resources.

Pencil Point # 6: You will have to have more than just an idea in order to approach a Pencil.

Pencil Point # 7: Product pricing is a strategic process and the highest price often is not the best price for the Pencil OR for you.

Pencil Point # 8: When planning product placement and pricing, do your research and bring in qualified help.

Pencil Point # 9: Don't attempt to meet with a Pencil until you are ready!

Pencil Point # 10: Plan your product launch around a logical progression of distribution, or risk becoming a casualty (or a not-for-profit organization).

Pencil Point # 11: Licensing can be tremendously rewarding but is not an amateur endeavor.

Pencil Point # 12: Pencils have alternatives to replace defensive, argumentative, and uncooperative suppliers.

Pencil Point # 13: Retailers are not responsible for your profitability!

Pencil Point # 14: When suppliers do their part, they become partners with their Pencils.

Pencil Point # 15: "No" means "Not yet" more often than you'd think.

Pencil Point # 16: Getting an appointment should be your first goal. Send samples in advance only if all else fails.

Pencil Point # 17: You can't hold your product samples so close that no one can see them, and you can't lose track of where they have gone. Fear of knock-offs will limit your options and can be a distraction from the real work that needs to be done.

Pencil Point # 18: Getting Pencil appointments takes patience, determination, and the ability to leverage success *and* rejection.

Pencil Point # 19: Playing by the rules and supplementing your direct contact efforts will greatly increase your chances of gaining a Pencil's interest.

Pencil Point # 20: Don't let your personal attachment to your idea lead to foolish hiring decisions, and if you can't afford to support a professional, qualified sales effort (yourself or an outside party), you should reconsider your venture.

Pencil Point # 21: Your Pencil prospects want to work with people who understand their business. Do whatever is necessary to find those people.

Pencil Point # 22: As a start-up, your first sell will be to top-notch sales representation. Swallow your ego and be willing to learn from those who know.

Pencil Point # 23: Working from a meeting plan makes the best use of time and increases the perception of your company's competence.

Pencil Point # 24: You didn't come this far to take shortcuts with preparation!

Pencil Point # 25: Involve your Pencil in the product development process while remaining mindful of your product's "reason to be."

Pencil Point # 26: Flexibility is the most important supplier quality in today's competitive environment.

Pencil Point # 27: Disorganized product presentations reflect poorly on your entire company, not just on the person conducting the presentation.

Pencil Point # 28: Don't wait to make investments in art, photos, computer-generated plan-o-grams, and other presentation aids. Many companies use these tools as a matter of course (and they may well be your competition)!

Pencil Point # 29: Regardless of your usual standards, those of your Pencil's office, and even casual Friday, keep an edge by strengthening your resolve to dress professionally!

Pencil Point # 30: Never treat anyone in the Pencil organization as a means to an end.

Pencil Point # 31: The more organized you are before your Pencil walks in, the more time you will have to show your products.

Pencil Point # 32: By the time line review rolls around, it should be easy for a Pencil to recall and write, based on your initial presentation and the materials you left behind.

Pencil Point # 33: The greeting is your first opportunity to demonstrate that you've done your homework.

Pencil Point # 34: Tell the Pencil who you are and why you are there.

Pencil Point # 35: Always strive to keep the Pencil meeting moving forward.

Pencil Point # 36: Being corrected can be the best thing that ever happened in a meeting. Don't waste energy trying to always be right or attempting to monopolize the dialog.

Pencil Point # 37: The end of your Pencil meeting is the time to ensure that you are moving in the right direction from that point forward.

Pencil Point # 38: The difference between firm orders and projections, forecasts, or estimates isn't necessarily the difference in who takes responsibility for inventory.

Pencil Point # 39: Understanding your Pencil's intentions for your product(s) is of utmost importance. You can then partner with them to maximize opportunities.

Pencil Point # 40: Pencils prefer that emails cut to the chase.

Pencil Point # 41: Create *standards* for communication and stick to them. Consistency counts!

Pencil Point # 42: Taking an intuitive and proactive approach with your Pencil will put you ahead of the pack.

Pencil Point # 43: Lack of response or slow response achieves nothing except to make your organization look unprofessional.

Pencil Point # 44: The memory of meetings will fade fast and you'll need to refer back to your notes more often than you think, especially as your business grows!

Pencil Point # 45: Documentation plays a huge role in today's retail environment. Leave nothing to chance and get everyone into the documentation habit.

Pencil Point # 46: Never demand buyer involvement. Work professionally and courteously with whoever is assigned to you.

Pencil Point # 47: Assistants become buyers. Treat them with respect!

Pencil Point # 48: All face-time with your Pencils provides an opportunity to demonstrate your professionalism, conflict resolution skills, product knowledge, and concern for your Pencil relationships. Meetings form the core of your company's overall business strategy. Don't waste a single opportunity by being reluctant, unprepared, or unprofessional.

Appendix 2. "Are You Really Ready for Retailers?" Checklist

Answer these questions before you meet with any Pencil!

- What is my capacity (how many of these items can I produce at a given time)?
- What is my current inventory (do I have any items on-hand right now and if so, how many)?
- What is my lead time (how quickly can I get items shipped to the Pencil and how many)? You'll want to know how low you can go in price negotiations while still making margin.
- What is my pricing structure (what is the lowest cost to the Pencil that I can offer while still making my desired margin)?
- Who will I be competing with within this retailer and what are my points of differentiation?

- If this item/items are not already in this retailer, what is my best guess as to why ("because they've never seen anything like this" is rarely the case)?
- What is the buying structure at my targeted retailers? Who buys what? (No two retailers are the same.)
- Which retailers do I have in mind for this product and why? "Because they have over 3,000 stores" is not a good answer!
- Do I understand which retailers are considered competition by the retailers I am targeting?
- What are the "reasons to be" for my product(s). What specific markets, needs/trends are being addressed?
- Am I prepared to offer this as an exclusive to a retailer? If not, who else will be seeing it?
- How will I facilitate orders (EDI capabilities, etc.)?
- Where is the shipping point for my product(s)?
- Where are they sourced?
- Do I have packaging capabilities?
- Can I execute pre-ticketing and special bar coding?
- Have my items been quality tested, or will they stand up to third-party quality testing?
- Have I thoroughly shopped the stores of my targeted retailers and devised a unique game plan for each one which refers to their current products, brands, fixturing, and pricing?
- Have I refilled my Xanax prescription? (Just joking!)

Glossary of Terms

Charge-Back - Form on which the amounts of merchandise returned to a retailer for credit or refund is recorded. Also, the amount that a retailer deducts from an invoice for various vendor infractions (late shipment, incorrectly marked containers, etc.).

Co-op Advertising - When advertising costs incurred by a retailer are divided between one or more supplier companies. Used to encourage promotion and advertising of particular products.

Cost - The amount a retailer pays a vendor for purchases.

EDI - Electronic Data Interchange. A system that enables retailers to integrate their purchasing activities with their stores and/or with vendors.

Line Review - A weeding out meeting between retail buyers and/or management in which competitive items for a given category or department are considered in context prior to making purchasing decisions. The line review process may be formal and corporately-mandated or an informal review between buyers and/or assistants.

PDQ - One of several terms that retailer use to describe pre-filled, pre-priced displays, provided by a vendor, that enable retail store personnel to quickly re-stock items without individual handling.

Plan-o-gram - A schematic drawing of fixtures that illustrate product placement. Also known as POG.

P.O. - Purchase order. A manually or electronically-generated authorization from a retailer to a supplier that signifies a retailer's intention to have specified quantities of products shipped to the retailer.

POS - Point of sale. Often used to refer to the number of units sold by a retailer.

RFID - Radio frequency identification, a technology similar in theory to bar code identification but with the capability of transmitting information continually regarding a product's specific qualities and location. Eliminates the need for line-of-sight reading that bar coding depends on and may be done at greater distances.

Index

About Our Firm

newmarketbuilders is a full-service business development and management-consulting firm that assists the consumer products industry with retail strategy and organizational readiness. newmarketbuilders builds on years of experience and success in the consumer products arena to help companies secure a long-term advantage in an increasingly competitive marketplace. Supplier companies utilize our services to assess and improve their market potential, new product and distribution opportunities, and retail and licensing relationships. Licensors and retailers call on us to improve their suppliers' sales strategy, market intelligence, and organizational readiness. newmarketbuilders builds relationships and increases productivity for our domestic and international client companies, including family-owned suppliers, consumer products companies, retailers, importers/exporters, and licensors/licensees. newmarketbuilders utilizes our understanding of the modern retail and licensing environment and major account sales processes to diagnose and clarify issues and risks, improve internal processes, increase supplier expertise, and create greater customer awareness.

newmarketbuilders is a woman-owned company, with offices in New York, NY, Denver, Colorado, and Bentonville, AR. Our firm is a member of *National Retail Federation, International Licensing Industry Association, Institute of Management Consultants, and Juvenile Products Manufacturers Association.*

Contact Information

If we can provide any additional information, please feel free to contact Carol Spieckerman or Lisa Carver by phone, email, post, or fax. Our contact information follows:

Mailing Address:

newmarketbuilders, inc. 771 South Oneida Street, Denver, CO 80224 U.S.A.

Telephone: 877.883.7647

Fax: 720.293.9977

Email: team@newmarketbuilders.com

Website: http://www.newmarketbuilders.com

For *Ready, Set ... Whoa! Are You Really Ready for Retailers?* reorders or to obtain other materials from the authors, please call toll-free 877.883.7647, extension 10.

About the Authors

Carol Spieckerman

Carol Spieckerman possesses over 20 years of experience with multi-million-dollar sales, sales management, new product launch, licensing, and business development. She brings high-volume, multiple S.K.U. sales and sales management experience with Wal-Mart, Target, J.C. Penney, Sears, the 'R Us group, food and drug stores, and better department and specialty stores to newmarketbuilders' clients.

Carol has built, managed, and motivated sales, product, and analytical teams for family-owned and corporate consumer products companies and driven exponential volume growth for those organizations. She has been charged with pioneering new business and procuring coveted high-volume accounts throughout her career and has become a "specialist" in addressing their needs.

Carol has played an integral strategic role within consumer products companies toward new product launches and line and brand extensions, and has served in a liaison role between supplier companies and their top licensors. She possesses a unique understanding of supplier/licensor/retailer dynamics as well as the increased need for customized approaches in the industry. Carol enjoys bridging the gap between suppliers and their customers via sales training, strategic hiring, and organizational solutions.

Lisa Carver

Lisa Carver has managed and implemented business development and marketing initiatives in the private and not-for-profit sectors since 1987. Working with both start-up and mature companies, Lisa has defined strategic growth initiatives and marketing strategies for consumer products and technology organizations while developing key global relationships in Asia Pacific, Canada, Mexico, and Europe.

Lisa works with consumer products executives to focus and position their companies for new product launches, acquisitions, and funding. Her specific experience in CRM, electronic commerce, and remote field data collection technologies helps newmarketbuilders' clients prepare for modern commerce.

Lisa's conflict resolution and intervention expertise has proven to be vital as companies make rapid and far-reaching organizational changes to remain competitive. She has developed key organizational messages as well as brand, identity, and media strategies to maximize exposure and has acted as a primary media liaison to broadcast and print media. She enjoys helping supplier companies fully realize the potential of existing resources and strengths and formulating long-range plans for strategic improvement. Lisa is a graduate of LIMA's inaugural Certificate of Licensing Studies program.